"I'd encourage all Christian ₁ children's decisions and navigate some of the challenging twists and turns in the lives of their daughters and sons to read this book by my friend, Carol Peterson. Her candor, stories, heartfelt prayers, and love for her children come alive in these pages. This story is at times heartbreaking, at times inspiring, but always hopeful—even in the valleys. It's a hope that is rooted in God's unfathomable love shone through a mother to her children, and what comes across even more is God's love for all of us."

—**Barry Corey, PhD,**
President of Biola University
Author of *Love Kindness: Discover the Power of a Forgotten Christian Virtue* and *Make the Most of It: A Guide to Loving Your College Years*

"Carol's story is not uncommon, as addiction among our children is prevalent all around us, but her story is interwoven with her steadfast faith in her Savior for herself and for her children. Throughout her story, she reminds herself and us who holds our future. The promises he gives us and the sustenance he gives to broken and hurting hearts when things have gone out of control are constant reminders we all need. As you read, be reminded of God's amazing grace. He is alive and active in the redemption of our hearts."

—**Michelle Bates,**
Author of *Beyond the Shallow—How Suffering Led Me to the Deep End of Grace*

Our Story

An Ordinary Family on an
Extraordinary Journey

Carol Peterson

 LUCIDBOOKS

Our Story
An Ordinary Family on an Extraordinary Journey

To my dearest grandchildren,
Elijah, Emilia, and Liberty.
You are loved.

Special Thanks

Sometimes the simplest words can have the most impact. Pastor Brian Minnich has often encouraged his congregation to simply "tell your story." When this book project loomed large, that encouraging refrain took root in my mind and heart.

Pastor Brian, thank you for believing I could muster through the writing of this book. Your unwavering support from the first drafts to the final stages never faltered. I am deeply grateful that you have partnered with my family and me in times of joy and in times of deep sorrow. Thank you, for joining us in the telling of our story.

Table of Contents

Preface

This book tells the story of one family's journey through the joys and stresses of raising children from their cherished early years through the tumultuous challenges of teenage chaos. We are ordinary church-going parents who have walked an extraordinary journey—one that we would never have envisioned for our family. Our story progresses from courtship to marriage to "normal" childrearing challenges to a harrowing struggle as two of our four children fall victim to drug addiction. Despite the challenges, this is a story of victory and overcoming in Christ; our story shows God's grace and mercy unfolding to bring beauty from ashes (Isa. 61:3).

Writing our story has been both emotionally challenging and healing. It is a work of passion, written from the depths of a mother's heart, with the guidance of the gentle and compassionate Holy Spirit. As I relived precious moments of joy and laughter and tears, I was reminded that the most important and valuable thread in our family's story is the love of Christ, which weaves through both the good and bad days.

It is my fervent hope that this story will encourage you whether your family is living through a similar struggle or whether you can use this as a cautionary tale to prepare for the time when your children begin to step out of the safety bubble of hearth and home. Unfortunately, many parents who are in similar situations struggle alone. I sincerely hope that reading about our journey through the ups and downs of life will speak hope for you and your family. Be assured that God is with you and that he is able to do more than you can imagine. Don't ever give up. Continue to put one foot in front of the other. Love your child fiercely because within that love lives hope.

This book offers a couple of unique features specifically designed to broaden its usefulness. First, addiction is a very complex issue affecting the individual as well as the family, so I chose to share multiple perspectives on our family dynamics as the situation evolved. Thus, various family members—husband and children—speak candidly throughout. Second, the book includes an appendix called "Questions for a Pastor" written by Brian Minnich, our church pastor. He writes from his heart as a parent, as a pastor, and as a Bible teacher. His question-and-answer section provides teaching, preventative measures for parents, and words of healing that I believe you will find invaluable.

Introduction

"Raising a child" is a basic definition for *parenting* according to *Merriam-Webster*. The job entails providing protection and care as children grow from helpless infants into productive adults. But this definition falls short: It tells us nothing about the stages of parenting or the journey involved or what to expect. Personally, I think some movie titles more accurately suggest the stages of parenting. The first year is typically characterized by the repetitiveness of *Groundhog Day* followed closely by the challenging years of the *Gremlins*. The teenage years are best classified as *Instructions Not Included* and *Mission Impossible*. All the years can be wrapped up in a beautiful bow that says *P.S. I Love You*.

During our first seven years together, my husband, Wayne, and I were blessed with four bouncing, happy babies. Together, we thrived with our children through the diaper and potty-training phases, succeeded in teaching little humans to color on paper instead of walls, and then advanced into adventures that inevitably led to emergency rooms for stiches and casts. We even survived the hair-raising phase of helping our children get their drivers permits and allowing them behind the wheel of our car. Through it all, God was there, always encouraging and teaching us.

Our family morphed from phase to phase while hanging onto the rollercoaster ride called life. We experienced the joys of the many firsts that parents treasure—those precious first smiles, first words, first friendships, and first accomplishments. In the beginning, I believed that parenting was most demanding when children were young and very needy. That was the phase when we didn't have a moment to ourselves—not even to sleep well. Exhaustion was our constant companion because infants and toddlers require continuous care, feeding, cleaning, and hugs. Day after day, the routine continued seemingly without end, but with the repetition and demands of this phase, we also experienced many threads of joy and the reassurance that God was with us.

We learned that each phase of parenting comes with its own set of challenges and rewards. When they became toddlers, our boys drove Matchbox cars furiously around the house, gleefully crashing into the furniture and each other. Eventually, they became teenagers and drove their first real cars into accidents. Thankfully, only the cars suffered injuries!

Our little girls grew from pretend princesses into truly beautiful brides. When it was their special day, their grooms looked on with adoration as each one made her way down the aisle on Dad's arm. Our flannel-clad boy grew into a handsome gentleman who later donned a tux and joined his lovely bride at the altar on their wedding day.

When he was three years old, our second son's favorite toy was his first two-wheeler. His short, sturdy legs would peddle furiously as he flew around and around on the driveway. Eventually, in his early twenties, with his mind altered by alcohol, he drove his brand-new motorcycle off the road. He narrowly missed impaling himself on the metal spears of a cemetery gate. Thankfully, his life was spared even as his body lay injured. Sadly, his little-boy hands that once clung to mine would, years later, inject a needle full of heroin into his veins for the last time.

Of all the struggles our family faced, the most difficult was the saga of drug addiction. Our experience with addiction began like a slow train that picked up speed until it careened out of control. Fear, anger, and hopelessness rode on this train with us. Despite the haze of destruction caused by addiction, a precious victory emerged as we sought refuge in God's Word:

> *Fear not, for I am with you; be not dismayed, for I am your God; I will strengthen you, will help you, I will uphold you with my righteous right hand.*
>
> —Isa. 41:10 ESV

I can testify today that his promises are true. Even with the unbelievable trauma and loss our family experienced, our story is one of a typical family, quite possibly similar to yours. More than ever, I can find peace in knowing that all our days are blessed as they are bound together with strong bonds of love. God was and still remains our strength and hope.

Chapter 1

In the Beginning

My house was quiet. It was well past my bedtime. I'm sure my parents didn't know that I had hidden the flashlight under my pillow beside my book. They believed I was sleeping. Instead, I read on and on deep into the night until my eyelids finally drooped with fatigue. The words started to blur, and my book finally closed. In that twilight moment, I said my prayers:

Dear God,

It's me again. I just wanted to let you know some things I've been thinking about. I've been thinking a lot about who I should marry and what my kids should be like. I'm sure you already know who my husband will be, but I wanted to let you know what I wanted.

My dream husband would be handsome and strong and have big muscles. Definitely not skinny! His eyes should be blue just like mine, so all our babies will

*have beautiful blue eyes and of course, he should have
blonde hair. He needs to be Finnish, and I don't like
any of the Finnish boys that I know, so you'll have to
find a different one. His hands are really important.
He has to have big, strong hands. I don't like wimpy,
limp hands on a guy. [I shuddered just thinking about
them.] Of course, Lord, you know what's best, so I
want the man you want for me but ... I love you, God.*

PS. He doesn't need to be rich. I'm not into big, fancy
things.

(Yep, I can't believe it either. I actually prayed to be poor!)
As a young girl, I considered simple rote prayers foolish. I meant
business when I prayed. My bedtime ritual included heart-to-
heart nightly discussions with God.

Prayers Answered

As it turns out, God listened, and he would give me all that I asked
for—and more. I love that God cares about the things that affect
us—both big and small.

The Lord dropped this hunk-of-my-dreams into my life at
a very young age. Wayne claims he first noticed me when I was
about 12 or 13 years old as he was sitting in the back row at church
with the guys. He said they were all talking and fooling around
when he spotted "this cute little blonde girl" sitting three or four
rows ahead of them. When I turned and looked back, Wayne says
he knew right away that I was going to be his wife.

He remembers that the other guys noticed me too and started
commenting, but he warned them all: "This one's going to be
mine, so you guys stay clear." At that point Wayne didn't think
I even noticed him. He was right. I didn't pick him out of the

line-up. All I noticed was a row of boys talking and laughing and that their attention seemed to be directed toward me. I squirmed uncomfortably in my seat and tried to ignore them although it crossed my mind that they were all kind of cute and blonde.

Several months plus a birthday passed before we finally met. Wayne was doing some "digging" within the youth group, trying to figure out how to meet "this cute, blonde girl." He had questioned everyone in the youth group before he finally connected with one of my sister's friends and convinced her to talk to my sister on his behalf. He asked her to bring me to the next church youth get-together at McDonalds. He said that while he waited, all he could think about was, "Carol . . . Carol . . . Carol."

The first time I remember becoming aware of Wayne was at my first big after-church youth outing at a McDonalds. Reluctantly, my sister had dragged me along. I remember that she said something ambiguous about a boy liking me. And that was it; I was on my own after getting to McDonalds.

I remember searching the group, trying to identify the mystery boy. Finally, I thought I had picked him out when I spotted an "older" guy like my sister had hinted; he was blonde and cute. However, he completely ignored me. He made no eye contact whatsoever—no effort to talk to me. Then to my astonishment, another boy suddenly sat down next to me and grinned at me and most likely introduced himself. I wasn't impressed—definitely not love at first sight. In fact, I decided to make a quick getaway.

Nonetheless, Wayne had left an impression that intrigued me, and the next time I saw him, I wasn't so quick to walk away. It wasn't long before he made my heart pound with his sweet baby blues and hair in shades of gold. But I think the turning point might have been when I noticed his hands. No small hands here. They were paws!

I wondered if he was aware of my eyes bugging out of my head at the sight of his large, strong, and calloused hands. Likewise, his wide, muscular shoulders made a huge impression. Pun intended! This guy was built. It was love at second sight. My youth group days had begun, and before long everyone knew the seat next to me was taken. By the time I turned 14, we started double dating because my father insisted that I have a chaperone. That turned out to be my big sister's job.

Talking Arja into chaperoning was not an easy feat. She had a life of her own, and it didn't include tagging along on her baby sister's fledgling romance. Enter Wayne's close cousin, Chan. Chan and Wayne were thick as thieves growing up together, so it made sense that Wayne would appeal to Chan to double date my sister and make it a foursome. After much persuasion, Arja finally agreed to go along with the scheme, and before long, no more persuasion was required. Unbeknownst to my dad, we left the house as a foursome but often found ways to become twosomes.

Our Foundation: Faith and Family

Growing up as Wayne and I had in a church pew, with faith-filled parents, had given us a rich heritage in God's Word. From a young age, I believed God was real. A fond memory for me is when I memorized the Beatitudes in Sunday School. For one week, I sat on our front step day after day, rehearsing out loud. The next Sunday, I stood bold and confident as I enunciated each Beatitude clearly for my Sunday School teacher. Yes, I earned the reward sticker, but something more important happened. A hunger for God's Word was birthed in me.

However, by the time I entered junior high school, I began my metamorphosis from a quiet, confident child into a painful intro-vert. The root cause of this transformation seemed minor, yet it proved to be extremely devastating. Blushing became the bane of my existence. It wasn't just a faint, light-pink flush that crept up my face. I could go from pale white to dark red tomato in two seconds flat.

I realized early on that when the teacher called on me to answer a question, even one I knew the answer to, my face would change color like a chameleon, and my brain would instantly turn off. The fear of blushing became a self-fulfilling prophecy, causing a daily recurrence. I soon decided that becoming invisible in the classroom was preferable to facing the taunts from peers about my color change. If you've struggled with a visible peculiarity, you know that it wreaks havoc with your self-esteem.

Church became my safe place, and Sunday services and youth group filled my tank, so I could get through the week. My youth group friends gave me the sense of confidence and acceptance that made it safe to be myself. Youth pastors reached out to me and made meaningful connections. I quickly realized that the triggers that caused me to turn into a "tomato" at school didn't exist in church. This freed me up to join the Sunday School teaching team, which opened up a whole new world for me. In that setting I was completely comfortable talking to a group—as long as the group was made up of children. Thus, my teaching career began at the age of 12.

Wayne was my polar opposite. He was boisterous and loud, not bothered at all if everyone in the room was listening to him. He often took on the big brother role for younger kids in our group. With Wayne around, no one lacked a ride to our fun events; anyone was welcome to jump into his already full car. I guess what they say is true: Opposites attract. That was certainly the case for us.

Underneath that carefree surface, however, Wayne sported his own "thorn in the flesh." My thoughts go back to the first time he invited me to his house. His nervousness was quite evident. He had told me about his Finnish-speaking grandfather who couldn't wait to meet the *little Finnish girl*. "He's going to want to talk to you. A lot! And in Finnish," Wayne warned me. That was totally fine with me. I looked forward to the conversation. True to his prediction, his grinning grandfather was standing on the stoop when we pulled into the driveway. He was talking to me long before I made it from the driveway to the steps. As our conversation continued, I started to follow him into the house. But Wayne interrupted.

"Not that way," he said. "This isn't my house. We live behind this house." His grandfather reluctantly let me pull away, but only after I promised that we would talk again. I followed Wayne around some bushes, and suddenly, before me stood a trailer. The trailer had an odd addition, which I can only describe as having a Frankenstein motif. This city girl who came from her white house with a picket fence was shocked. Incredulously, I thought: *"Someone actually lives in there?"* I was soon to discover that a *lot* of people actually lived in there!

Wayne Speaks

Embarrassment! A deep-seated mortification that I couldn't escape. That's what I felt all my childhood. I hated where we lived. I hated how we lived. I spent every minute I could away from that house. I hated bringing Carol home to my house. We were poor. We were poorer than poor. We ate government food. My father drove cars that were scrapped by other people. He'd keep them going until he couldn't. Then I'd drive them through the backyard, over the wooden plank bridge into the woods.

That's where I spent a lot of my time from about the age of 8. I learned to tinker with those cars, keeping them running. I spent hours driving them around the track I created in the back woods. It was my private hideaway.

I hoped I schooled my expression of shock as I followed Wayne inside the trailer. To my surprise, the trailer seemed to fall away as I saw his parents' welcoming smiles. The house was filled with action and motion. I learned over the years that this house was a *home*—a home filled with love, laughter, and acceptance.

Years later, Wayne still says, he couldn't believe people wanted to come to his house. "Our house was always filled with people; they would pop in at all times of the day or night. It didn't matter whether it was two in the morning; the coffee pot was always on. My parents would be up and ready for company. There was always room and time for you."

When I first met his large family, my jaw dropped. I had never seen a house with so many kids. His family was a cacophony of voices and bodies in perpetual motion. The dynamics of a household the size of Wayne's was a new phenomenon to me since I have only one sibling. It was a delight to go to his house just to sit on the couch and watch the show. The dynamics of the sibling pecking order playing out in Wayne's home was fascinating. The siblings were boisterous and loyal though at times, they were embroiled in friendly scrapes.

My small nuclear family was the opposite of Wayne's large tribe. I came from a serious-minded, tranquil family of four. The pecking order in my home was quite clear-cut: I was the younger child, and my sister Arja held the leadership role whereas in Wayne's house, the loudest and strongest ruled the moment. However, it was very evident that close bonds of love knit together both his family and mine.

In our high school years, Wayne and I lived for the weekends when our church group got together. Our youth group was called Christ Ambassadors. (A big shout out to all former CAs!) Do you remember rock-a-thons? Adults actually paid us to rock in rocking chairs all night. All the proceeds went to missions. We were constantly raising money for Speed the Light, a missionary outreach of our denomination. I still remember the nausea and rocking that continued in my head when I finally climbed into bed sometime around eight o'clock in the morning. Those were fun-filled nights. These memories are awesome blasts from the past of youth activities that gave us a sense of purpose and kept us safe from choices that could have taken us down a darker path.

During my high school years, I never lacked for a date. I always had my steady beau at my side. His proposal came on Christmas Eve right before my 18th birthday. Our tradition was to celebrate Christmas Eve with my parents and Christmas Day with his parents. That year, he walked in the door with a beautiful bouquet of roses and placed them under the tree. I immediately went to pick them up to put them in water, but he stopped me, telling me they were his present to be opened later. I was a bit miffed because I thought they would wilt.

But all my annoyance fled when he popped the question after dinner, kneeling on one knee near the Christmas tree. My engagement ring was attached to the stems of the roses! Of course, my answer was yes; however, I had one stipulation. We would have to wait until I graduated with my associate degree two years later.

Chapter 2

Double Dating Leads to Double Happiness

Our wedding morning dawned bright and beautiful on May 17, 1980. Our wedding would take place at our home church with family and friends gathered to celebrate with us. The organist would play the traditional wedding march. It was to be traditional in every sense of the word except one: My father would walk two brides down the aisle, one on each arm. On that day, Arja's and my years of double dating would turn into a double wedding ceremony. Because we had brought them together years before, Wayne and I were proud to take full credit for the future Mr. and Mrs. Chan Kangas.

Many people were surprised by our decision to have a double wedding. Somewhat shocked, several people asked, "Don't you want your own wedding day?" The answer was simply no. Arja and I had shared a bedroom, clothing, makeup, and many laughs and tears growing up. It was only natural that we would share a very special date—our wedding day. And we were marrying cousins, so the groom's side of the church was filled with one family, and the bride's side of the church was filled with one family. What could be more blessed than having two families share a wedding day?

Thankfully, the family members and friends in those pews waited patiently when the brides were beyond fashionably late. The morning at the brides' home had begun exactly as planned. The two brides, the six bridesmaids, and the two flower girls, along with helpful family members gathered right on schedule. Finally, with hairdos just right, makeup expertly applied, and zippers zipped perfectly, it was time for treasured photos. The photographer worked quickly and efficiently snapping glorious shots. Then someone shouted, "It's getting late, we have to go!" Everyone rushed out of the house and piled into cars and sped away—everyone, that is, except the two brides!

We were left behind in the confusion of the moment. I'll have to admit to panic. We didn't have a car. This was before cell phones. All we could do was wait and wait and wait longer, hoping that someone would notice our absence and come back for us. Which didn't happen. Later, we learned that everyone at church thought we had my sister's car. Which we didn't. After what seemed forever, the phone rang. Friends traveling from out of town called in the hope that someone could give them directions to the church. Providentially, they were lost and couldn't find the church. They had the totally unexpected privilege of bringing the brides to the wedding.

With that challenge overcome, the wedding went off without a hitch. The bridesmaids walked in unison down the aisle. A chorus of "Oohs and Aahs" was heard as the adorable flower girls and sweet ring bearers hesitantly made their way to the altar. Then came the moment everyone had been waiting for: The long-awaited brides made their appearance at the entrance—one wearing a veil, the other a hat. Each bride wore a dress that was unique and beautiful. Our solemn dad walked us down the aisle to join our handsome grooms who were wearing black tuxedos with matching shiny patent leather shoes. Well, except for one of the grooms who had ditched his patent leather shoes for his comfortable, well-worn brown shoes. Can you guess which groom that was?

God had blessed me with the man of my dreams, and we learned the value of hard work together. The bonus in this marriage was that I gained nine new brothers and sisters.

Our First House

After our wedding, Wayne and I bought a 100-year-old farmhouse in our hometown on Cambridge Street. In its glory days, the house had been surrounded by a large apple orchard. As years passed, the city crept in, and the apple orchard disappeared. The house had been transformed from a single-family home into a tenement house. When we moved in, the house stood watch on top of its small hill, and instead of overlooking apple trees, it watched as cars and trucks rumbled by day and night.

The old farmhouse was surrounded by other three-decker tenement houses, which had transformed the orchard into an inner-city neighborhood. When we purchased this home, its small footprint contained two rented studio apartments on the first and second floors with a significantly larger attic apartment on the third floor. As newlyweds, we moved into the shabby but functional and cozy third-floor apartment.

Over the decades that we lived in the farmhouse, we could have produced several home rehab TV specials. Our first rehab project involved reconfiguring the entire third floor. We moved in with Arja and Chan while Wayne gutted and rebuilt the apartment from its studs. After several months, we moved back into the transformed space, which was the perfect size for our small family of three. A year later, we easily fit in baby number two. Our next rehab projects included removing dingy popcorn ceilings and replacing cracked horsehair plaster walls in the studio apartments. Eventually, we swapped out drafty windows with cracked sills for new window panes. Then we painted the house a lovely charcoal gray. As we took care of this old house, she became a safe haven for our family and for many other hurting people who came through her doors.

Building a Foundation for Our Family

Wayne and I began wedded bliss as a poor working-class couple. Our early years were lean. We lived paycheck to paycheck. Although our house was on the wrong side of the financial tracks, over the next decade we both dug in and applied our God-given spirit of tenacity and bulldog determination to improve our situation. Wayne combined his skills with an entrepreneurial spirit and opened his own hardwood floor company.

The odds of success were strong against a small startup company, but Wayne didn't let that stop him. One night he turned to me pleased as punch and said, "I've been doing something different. I started praying down my contact list on my phone for all my contractors and customers. And work is pouring in." Thus, began his phone prayer list, which he has maintained for decades. For years now, Wayne has seen the blessing of a steady stream of customers, and his waiting list is consistently four to five months out. The contractors who began working with Wayne when he started praying for his customers and his business have become the backbone of his company.

I joined in on Wayne's entrepreneurial spirit and opened my own home day care. As with most businesses, this meant researching rules and regulations, meeting state and local codes, and applying for a license. Several blessings came to us during this time to give us a financial boost. From the beginning, my day care was always at capacity. Children came from either church families or an organization called Saint Agnes Guild. The Guild connected me to a government food program that covered groceries for the day care and my own children. The only requirement was for me to keep a log of the nutritious food served. Although we were not making large paychecks, our income always covered the bills. Year after year, God has proven that we do not need to be anxious about what we will eat or drink, the clothes we wear, or the roof over our heads. Our heavenly father knows our needs and meets them all.

Chapter 3

Blessings of Children

Over a seven-year period, we became parents to four blue-eyed, blonde-haired towheads. God's direct answer to my prayer was the gift of two energetic boys followed by two lovely girls.

First to arrive on the scene was Corey, our brave and fearless child. As a rambunctious climber, he sported a permanent bruise in the middle of his forehead for at least the first seven years of his life. What would you think of a child's parents if you were standing in a church parking lot and saw a six-year-old at the top of a light pole? You'd probably have an anxiety attack like several lovely churchgoers who stood gasping one Sunday morning as Corey shimmied up a light pole. Wayne stood at the bottom of the pole chuckling and calling out encouragingly.

I came upon this scene when Corey was already halfway up the pole. I had to stop yelling at Wayne because by the time Corey scooted up to the light, I wasn't breathing anymore. The thought crossed my mind: *If I keep yelling, I might cause Corey to fall.* Corey actually waved to us once he made it all the way to the top!

My heart finally started beating again as he gleefully slid down the pole like a fireman. I have to admit to a small "proud mama" moment. How many mamas can say their son can climb to the top of a light pole at age six?

"There wasn't anything I could do," Wayne recalls of this incident. "Corey just ran over to the pole and started climbing. I knew he could do it, so I wasn't worried. Anyway, I was standing right underneath and could've caught him had he fallen. I just wish I'd had a smartphone, so I could have caught it on camera." Oh, my goodness! There really wasn't anything more I could say, was there?

During summer kids camp, Corey became well-known for his flagpole-climbing skill. When the flag became tangled, they just called him over. In front of the whole camp, he would scoot up the pole to untangle the flag. Before scooting back down, he would take time to look out over the crowd—most likely grinning down from his perch!

In elementary school, the gymnastic team became the outlet for Corey's boundless energy and daredevil skills. I received several frantic calls from teachers over the years: "Could you please tell Corey that cartwheels and flips are not allowed during recess? Other kids might emulate him and end up getting hurt. Also, could you tell him to walk on his feet, not his hands?" He thought it was totally acceptable to walk handstand-style down the hallway or up the stairs. *What trouble could that cause?* I'm sure these stunts caused quite the spectacle, at least for a few minutes. It was hard to take these concerns too seriously. I was actually very proud of Corey's gymnastic abilities.

Fifteen months after Corey's birth, his younger brother Timothy joined our family in 1985. He was our soft-hearted "Michelin Tire" baby. He had rolls on top of rolls, which made him the most cuddlesome baby ever, and he had a smile that melted your heart. Best of all, he loved great big bear hugs, whereas Corey was too busy for such frivolous things. Timmy followed his big brother and cousin Ben into many feats of mischief. However, he also had a sensible sense of fear, which kept him mostly on the ground with a few exceptions.

During winter storms, Corey boldly coaxed his younger brother into jumping off the second-floor porch into snow piles. Lisa, our third-floor tenant at the time, remembers her panic as she watched the two boys sail over the railing. She didn't know they had created a mountain of snow below the porch. Who do you think was the instigator of this fun adventure? That would be Dad, of course.

Not to be left out of the daredevil stunts, Timothy joined Corey and his cousin Ben snowboarding and skateboarding. All three found hanging in the air and speeding over snow moguls or wooden ramps thrilling. Along the way, we graced several emergency rooms for stiches and casts.

Even as a young child, Timmy had a deep concern for others as evidenced by several treasures stashed away in my Bible. One such treasure is a note from Christmas 1993 written by Timmy when he was eight years old. It reads, *"Dear Mom, I love you very much and I hope you have a nice Christmas you are very specil to me you make me super, dinner, and lunch. Love Timmy."* His teacher had given the class an assignment to print a card. His ink-drawn picture on the front showed our house with two trees on either side; he was so very proud of his work.

Timmy was a giver. When his grandmother passed away at the age of 84, we found small pictures he had drawn just for her. She had kept them in her collection of special things since he was about seven or eight years old. That reminds me of the assortment of Christmas gifts Timmy gave me over the years—my all-time favorite is a Bible verse rolodex. It lives on my bathroom windowsill, and every morning, I turn it to the day's verse. Timmy was a young man of few words, but his actions spoke for him: He was always a giver.

Three years after Timmy was born, Tanja, our socialite, made her entrance. I had picked out her name when I was a very young girl. We rejoiced at her birth. Finally, we had our "Tanja." Tanja never met a stranger. She loved everyone from the minute she realized there were people in her small world. She'd hold her hands out to anyone who would talk to her. Her smile and infectious giggles lit up the room.

As a toddler she personified her favorite song by Carly Simon: "You Are My Sunshine." Her body would begin to sway, and her whole face would light up whenever she heard the first line. And the sunshine would spread rapidly to all who joined in singing the chorus. Tanja's social personality became one of her strongest attributes in school. Her cheery demeanor drew peers and teachers alike. She effortlessly developed friendships and kept a strong, close-knit group of friends.

While the boys were busy with stunts, Tanja joined the drama club and took on lead roles. I remember being so fascinated by her performance in one of her high school plays. She memorized an unbelievable number of lines while bringing her character to life. But her strongest attribute always was and continues to be her kind and humble heart.

Victoria, our serious and studious child, completed our family in 1991. She was the exact opposite of Tanja. She was shy and quiet, and social interactions made her uncomfortable. By the time Victoria was born, our house was full of day care children and neighborhood friends. Even when surrounded by others, Victoria could remain an island unto herself. As the youngest, she had to stay in the yard when her older siblings were allowed to take off into the neighborhood. It can be tough being the baby of the clan. Tanja often included Vicky in her world, and the two sisters developed a beautiful, close relationship. Tanja became a little mom, looking after her baby sister.

By the time Victoria started preschool, her white, blonde hair had finally grown enough to be pulled up into a "tree" on top of her head. This was her first signature hairdo. This fourth child shared my passion for reading. She learned to read early, and books became her favorite companion. But as much as she loved to read, books came in second place to her true passion. Victoria was devoted to another love: cats. She seemed to find stray cats everywhere. You could call her the pied piper of cats. She brought them home regularly, begging us to keep each one. She would beg and plead their plight as if they were doomed if she didn't rescue them.

We'd explain that the cats most likely belonged to someone and insist she let them go home. But then she changed her strategy. Instead of cats, she started bringing home tiny kittens. Who can say no to a kitten? Certainly not me. The craziest thing is that I used to do exactly the same thing as a young girl. Sometimes, her strategy worked, but most of the time, it didn't.

Thanks to Victoria, our family had a succession of beloved cats. They were all named "Kitty," and they were all black. Unfortunately, they usually met the same fate when they ventured onto the busy street in front of our house and subsequently went to the cat graveyard in our back woods. Corey's friend Shawn was our impromptu minister who volunteered to perform the ceremony for the last "Kitty." He did a marvelous job of saying final words of comfort. To this day, Victoria is a devoted pet mommy.

Sowing Seeds of Faith for a Lifetime

A mother's job is a daunting one, for sure. There are always hungry stomachs to fill, dishes to wash, a house to keep in order, scrapes and bruises to kiss, and unseen hurts-of-the-heart to repair. More importantly, as parents, we have a high calling to plant seeds of faith and godly knowledge in our children's hearts and minds. From the beginning, Wayne and I realized that our kids needed more than just "mom and dad's" religion; they needed to build their own relationship with God.

As I read Jesus's parable of the sower (Matthew 13:1–9), I see parallels with a parent's role in raising children. In the parable, the farmer sows or scatters seeds all over the ground. It's interesting to me that he doesn't sow seeds systematically as we might think a farmer would. At first glance, that seems rather foolish to me. I have to ask, "Why would he spread the seeds on rocks and dry ground?" But when I put myself in the role of the farmer, I see myself casting seeds of God's truth over my children. When they were growing up, the seeds I cast were words and actions meant to guide and protect, and I prayed that my children would blossom into healthy adults in body, mind, and spirit. Like the farmer, my job was to sow the seeds, water, and till the ground. I spread those seeds throughout the days and seasons of their lives whether the skies were prosperous and sunny or dark and dreary. My job was not to judge the condition of the soil, my children's hearts and minds. Often the farmer is amazed by the crop that grows, not just in the rich soil, but also in the most unlikely place. Wearing my mom hat meant that I taught my children many life lessons— lessons about sharing and kindness, starting when they were toddlers. As my children grew, so did the character lessons they were taught.

As parents, we recognized that seeds of faith are not only sown by us, so we tapped into the wisdom of positive adult influences for our children. Our small band of teenagers needed a community where they could mature in their humaneness, wrestle with theology, and grow in a personal and genuine walk with God. As the kids grew, Wayne and I worked toward the goal that all of our household would develop a faith that sticks. During their formative years, we made sure our children were involved in Thursday night youth group and weekend church activities as we had been. I thank God for the spiritual leaders who gave of themselves to lay foundations of biblical truth for our children. Those leaders played an important role in building our children up to be the strong adults they are today.

In addition to the seeds sown by our church family, Wayne and I were blessed to have the help of two sets of grandparents in raising our family. These grandparents played many precious roles for our children. Grandma Peterson was the great storyteller. She charmed her grandchildren with tales and affection. Grandpa Marlow (Wayne's dad) made everyone feel loved and important with his gentle smile and big bear hugs. Sadly, he left us much too early and is greatly missed by his family and friends.

Pappa (my father) played his accordion and sang hymns for anyone who would listen. Mummu (my mother) baked and prayed. She felt the need to feed all the grandchildren. Best of all the grandparents were always ready to babysit at the drop of a hat.

There is something very special about the love of grandparents. Their strongest influence can be found in the legacy they leave behind—a legacy of a life of hope lived with Christ. Their prayers for their children and grandchildren continue even though they have gone home.

Chapter 4

Our Little House Becomes a Gathering Place

When we first settled in the neighborhood on Cambridge Street, I wondered how anyone could survive in this part of the city—clearly this was the "wrong side of the tracks." The tenement houses were run down; some had graffiti on the walls. Some people dressed in rags or the opposite, clothing that made a statement. Sometimes, I saw people stumbling down the streets or hanging out brooding at the street corners while other pedestrians kept their heads down as they hurried to their destinations. Driving through the area flooded me with a myriad of unfamiliar and uncomfortable feelings. I wondered how anyone survived in this part of the city. It was so different from my maple tree-lined streets with well-kept homes and lush green yards.

In time, I learned that the wrong-side-of-the-tracks could be a blessing and a source of growth for Wayne and me. I thank God for changing my narrow mindset and growing me in compassion and humility. It was here that we met "Albie," a hard-working Polish immigrant neighbor who kept an eye out for the safety of the whole street and particularly our family. He came to consider himself an honorary grandfather to our children. Our lives were enriched by many special neighbors like Albie who persevered through hardships. On this street, we were part of a community. As neighbors, we looked out for each other, greeted each other with smiles and waves, and learned each other's names. This side of the tracks became the foundation on which to build our lives and future.

Building Friendships

Our children never lacked for friends to play with. Children poured out of the triple-decker apartment houses, resembling a swarm of ants taking over the street where pick-up games of baseball sometimes hampered traffic on our street and carried on well after sunset. A favorite hangout spot was our tire swing which hung in a small crop of trees. These trees included a great attraction for onlookers, Corey's tree house.

Of course, Corey couldn't keep his feet on the ground. He worked industriously to build and rebuild an intriguing fort in the sprawling branches above the tire swing. This fort was made from an interesting collection of recycled and refurbished materials. Everyone gazed in wonder when he dragged up the old passenger seat from Wayne's permanently parked box truck that served as a shed. Corey managed to secure it and sat high up in his tower. Well actually, it wasn't all that high, but it was magnificent in a ragtag way.

I am not sure whether Victoria and her friends were afraid to climb the tree or whether they were not allowed in the tree house. But the younger girls decided to be creative as well. They produced a much simpler deck on the box truck, parked conveniently near the tree. Typically, after many hours of adventure, hunger was the driving force that caused the swarm to head back into the triple-decker apartment houses.

The whole gaggle of neighborhood friends and cousins had orchestrated many shenanigans by the time they hit their stride in their early teens. Serious games of manhunt were extended well into the night hours. Children romped through the backyards and between the triple-deckers throughout the neighborhood. This was sometimes met with angry shouts from elderly neighbors who did not appreciate the shrieks of children playing games in their backyards. Manhunts escalated to a new level when our rascals started sneaking out of the house after lights out. Since every floor had its own exit, it was very easy to get out without Wayne and me knowing what was going on.

Truthfully, it was just more relaxing for us to pretend we didn't know what they were up to sometimes. In the early days, I wasn't worried about these departures; their play was innocent and adventurous. We trusted our kids.

Besides the creaky backdoor, the bathroom window became an escape hatch onto the back porch. Sometimes, I even used the escape hatch in reverse to get into the house if I forgot my keys. Our front door was very easy to break into with a credit card, but I happened to be the only family member who didn't have that skill.

Shawn, Corey's high school buddy, was the prime instigator of some crazy, clandestine midnight missions; he became the Robin Hood of the clan. Shawn always had a mischievous glint in his eye along with his charming smile. His daredevil attitude earned him the role of ringleader with Tanja and her gregarious girlfriends. Tanja remembers the fun would always begin with a movie night on the third floor with the guys. Before long Shawn would have one of his brilliant ideas.

Tanja Speaks

Shawn called himself the grandfather, and he had a mission. He wanted to take us on adventures so we would have fun stories to tell our grandkids someday. One of his schemes was "roofing." There were three factories in our neighborhood that we would visit on a regular basis. Often this happened somewhere around two in the morning. We would use the fire ladders to get up on the roofs of the factories. Sometimes, Shawn had to boost us up to the ladders. Then, on the roof, we'd all lay on our backs and watch the stars.

One time, the cops pulled up. We saw the blue lights, and we thought they were there for us. But instead we laid on our stomachs and watched them arrest some guy below on the sidewalk. They had no idea we were up on the roof. Roofing wasn't our only nighttime adventure. Our huge neighborhood cemetery proved to be a great midnight playground. In one of those missions, we stole fire extinguishers from trucks behind a warehouse in our neighborhood. Next, we all proceeded to the largest of the two city cemeteries down the street. Using the fire extinguishers, we played a crazy game of tag among the tombstones in the dark.

The next day, I wore the same sweatshirt to school as I'd worn that night. I fell asleep in math class. I had my head on the desk when the teacher came up behind me and tapped me on the shoulder. A white puff of powder billowed off my sweatshirt all over his hand.

Discovering an Unexpected Ministry

The lyrics of *"Our House"* by Crosby, Stills, and Nash seems to fit life on Cambridge Street. Our house became a refuge, a place where people were welcome and found rest. It was a place of acceptance and support when life turned hard. Our lives in this home unfolded into an unexpected ministry. Over the years, many people found refuge or a place to regroup in our apartments. A steady flow of singles, couples, and families came and went through the years. In all these encounters, the biggest change was not the rehab of our house but of our hearts. Cambridge Street was home for many, and our tenants became our lifelong friends, our sisters and brothers. We shared the treasured gift of months and sometimes years together.

When we bought the little farmhouse, it came fully furnished with tenants. Over time, those tenants moved out, and we were hesitant to advertise. How could we trust people we didn't know? It turned out that we didn't need to seek tenants. They showed up—one after the other every time an apartment became vacant. One of our first new tenants was a single woman from church who was trying to make ends meet. She had been hesitant to rent from someone she didn't know, so she was grateful to find an apartment with us. Another tenant was a man who worked with Wayne. His small family lost their apartment, and they were desperate. Then, came a string of newlyweds who were starting their dreams of a future together, but money was tight. We felt it was our calling to keep the rents low and affordable. Even in times when it seemed impossible for us to stretch our own funds to pay bills, our financial needs were met. Finally, when an apartment became vacant, we got excited and looked forward with anticipation to see who would walk in our doors next.

Our meager budget was stretched even further when we opened our doors without the expectation of receiving rent. There were those whose needs superseded ours. By this time, we were living on the first floor where we had combined the two studios into one apartment. The two second-floor studios and the third-floor apartment became our rentals.

The most humbling and precious people who walked through our doors were those living through tragedies and needing a place to shelter during the storm. Our first such tenant was a dear friend fleeing a dangerous altercation with her husband. A second-floor studio became a safety net for her and her two children while she prayed and planned her next steps. Our hearts were broken when another dear friend, a mother of five young children, passed away unexpectedly from a heart condition. Her husband and children moved into one of our second-floor apartments, and my day care gained toddler twins. The father transferred the older children to the same school as our children, and he was able to continue working to support his family. We had the honor of loving this family as they regained a sense of stability.

Another set of move-ins couldn't rightfully be called tenants. A neighbor, the mother of a friend of our boys, knocked at our door. She had a desperate look in her eyes as she asked to come in. We knew that this mom was fighting a drug addiction, but we were not prepared for what she asked when she sat at our table. She explained that she had been mandated into a drug rehab program for a full year, and she asked whether we would take her two children in to live with us. If we didn't step in, the children would go into foster care for the year. That day we gained our third son and a teenage daughter. For the next year, we were a family of eight.

The configuration of our house continued to evolve as our family grew. As a family of eight, we had to combine apartments with some very creative design plans. We already had our two boys sharing a bedroom and our two girls sharing another very small space. All the apartments were connected by a hallway staircase in the front of the house. This was great for privacy, but it wouldn't work if a second-floor studio became children's bedrooms. Fortunately, the studio above our bedrooms was vacant at the time. Imagine that! In a small bedroom in our apartment, Wayne cut a square in the ceiling. Then he proceeded upstairs and cut an opening in the mini-kitchen floor above. Viola! We had an opening the size of a person. The final creative touch was an old wooden ladder. And just that simply, we had an extra stairway leading to our new upstairs bedrooms. The kids in the neighborhood thought we were the coolest house on the block!

When the boys became older teens, it was harder to fit everyone into our existing bedroom configuration. Eventually, we took over the whole triple-decker. No more tenants. By this time the list of teens living with us had grown quite large. The third floor became the boys' apartment. It turned into a home to many friends, sometimes for just a few nights, and often for several months at a time. Our house continued to resemble the house of the old woman who lived in a shoe. Beds were made up in every room including the large third-floor closet.

With so many people coming and going, a neighbor asked whether we had converted our house into a rooming house. I loved our constantly growing family. We never wanted to turn anyone away because life can be hard—and harder yet for teenagers. Adolescence was a chaotic and traumatic time for many of the teens who called me their surrogate mom. Raising four kids was hard enough, but we often doubled that number under our roof.

Chapter 5

Summertime Memories

In the summertime, a rustic cottage at a nearby lake became an extension of our home. Every summer, we packed everything into our van except the kitchen sink, in order to spend several weeks at the lake. Excitement was tangible in the tightly packed van as we bounced down the rutted dirt road toward the campsite, which had three enticing, no frills, rustic cabins. Each year, we made the trek to the lake with eager anticipation. As the road broke into the clearing near the cottages, a glimmering lake popped into view, and a few hundred yards down the hill, adventures we had dreamed about since the previous year awaited the whole family.

The small private beach was a godsend. Every summer, the kids swarmed like ants over the small mountain of fresh sand dumped in the corner of the beach. Friendly sand-castle-building competitions abounded. When the kids were all very young, Uncle Chan scattered coins in the sand, and the kids took turns using a metal detector to find them.

Victoria Speaks

Like most kids, I waited in anticipation for the end of the school year and the start of the summer. My most prominent summer getaway memories are of our camping weeks at the lake. As a kid, I would spend all day by the lake, swimming and looking for snakes and frogs along the shoreline. The nights were spent making s'mores by the glowing embers of the fire while nursing a fresh sunburn. The lake was my childhood paradise, my home away from home. The small, secluded cabin in the woods offered all of us a much-needed escape from the city.

At night, the cottage loft was packed with kids like a sardine can. Wayne and I encouraged our kids to invite all their friends for a massive sleepover that lasted all week. The best was when the aunts, uncles, and cousins took the other two cottages, and our families "owned" the whole campsite.

The kids' days were spent swimming, boating, fishing, and looking for treasure while parents played lifeguard and camp cook. The boys commandeered the fishing boats from early morning to evening while the girls got the old run-down wooden rowboat.

Tanja Speaks

The boat was in awful shape. However, that didn't stop my cousin Elena and me from using it. It was our only option. We would raid all three cabins for the best snacks. Stealthily, we'd load them into the rowboat and be gone all day out on the lake. We had the best times when Timmy didn't go out in the fishing boat and joined us in the rowboat instead. He would tie a rope to the back of the boat and take us tubing. Rowing steadily, he pulled us leisurely around the cove. We rocked madly when the speed boats created big waves. It wasn't a very fast ride, but we loved it.

Those boats made for many happy days on the lake. When Corey was about ten, he announced that he would be camping out in the woods that year instead of sleeping in the loft. Wayne and I didn't imagine that he would last even one night before aborting his plan, but he surprised us both and made it through the entire week.

Corey Speaks

My older cousin told us about hunting. I was intrigued. I loved the woods. I decided if I was going to be a hunter I had to face my fears. I was afraid to be alone in the dark in the woods. I thought to myself, "What's the best way to get rid of fears?" I decided the answer was to face them. I hatched a plan to set up a campsite in the woods for the week.

And that's exactly what I did. I carried a pup tent and my sleeping bag out to a spot that I thought was deep in the woods. Looking back, I realize it was only about 100 yards away from the cabin. I pitched my tent in a dense tree area and then covered it completely with branches. I camouflaged it well.

Every night, after the bonfire, I followed the ray from my flashlight to my tent. Listening to the summer night sounds, my fears departed. The woods are where I find my solace even now; the times we had at the cabin

were the best times of my young life. It was my escape
from the city to the woods where everything felt right.

As the kids grew older, my sister and I enjoyed pulling some
pranks during the summer trysts to the lake. On one such night,
while all the kids were fast asleep, we couldn't resist heading up to
the loft. Silently, we drew a silly face on each of the girl's bellies.
Then we borrowed the girls' nail polish and painted the boys'
toenails a hot pink. They were so tired from being out on the boats
all day that they all slept through the prank.

When they awoke in the morning, they took the joke with good
grace. I think Joe, one of the boys' friends, laughed the hardest.
The boys even turned down the offer of nail polish remover, and
instead, enjoyed their colorful toes. Tanja still chuckles over the
memory. "I thought it was hilarious," she said; "Joe had hot pink
nails for the rest of the week!"

Just this year, Joe popped in on Mother's Day with flowers
and chocolates for me. He and his wife are now parents of two
beautiful children of their own. Joe has a big, loving heart, and he
came to give me bear hugs and gifts. All the children who walked
through our doors will forever be my adopted sons and daughters.

Back on Cambridge Street, our home was hopping. There was
never a dull day to be found. All moms know what stress a house
full of kids can bring on. As much as I pretended to be super mom,
I knew I wasn't. Mistakes and missteps are par for the course, so I
often found myself praying from the depths of my heart:

Lord,

I need you today. Guide me to live out your love in
front of these children each day. Help me to be wise
with small and big problems. Lord, let them hear your
voice in mine. Forgive me when I fail, which seems to

be often. In my own strength, this job is too big for me. But I trust you to take care of that which you have given to us. Above all, let them all learn to love you.

Amen.

Chapter 6

Youth Group and Missions

Youth group brought community, comradery, and even challenges for our children. Our rule was that anyone could sleep over, but if that evening or the next morning was a church day, then everyone in the house went to church with us. Within the hallowed walls of church, my children heard the Word of God spoken, saw worship, and sometimes chose to participate—one child even fell through a church ceiling!

Yep, you read that correctly. During one of the all-night youth events, unsuspecting leaders thought the kids would have fun playing hide-and-seek. My group of boys had no trouble climbing into the rafters to hide. Unfortunately, Timmy stepped on a ceiling tile that had no support. He crashed through the ceiling into the hallway below, leaving a huge hole in his wake. Wayne got a call from the associate pastor that night. In his somber, pastoral voice, he told Wayne that he had "a ceiling to come fix." And of course, that's exactly what Wayne did. Needless to say, that was the last time the youth group was allowed to play hide-and-seek.

It's a little ironic that Wayne's dad had to fix a church ceiling when Wayne was in his early teens. Wayne had pulled the same maneuver in his youth group days and put his foot through the church ceiling—directly over the pulpit. Wayne and his dad worked through the night fixing the ceiling before morning service. The apple didn't fall far on that one.

Tanja's socialite personality bloomed in her teen years. She never lacked for the close friendship of a gaggle of girls. She was a magnate for quiet and reticent girls who needed a friend as well as for girls who were comfortable in their own skin.

Throughout the years, our church has partnered in mission trips with an organization called Book of Hope. We were thrilled when Tanja was able to take part in two of these wonderful opportunities. Her first trip was to Guatemala.

Tanja Speaks

Two of my best friends joined me on the mission trip to Guatemala. We bubbled with enthusiasm during the fundraising and preparation stage. Our high energy level kept us chatting nonstop during the flight. Together, we were courageous, and we were anticipating a great time on this strange, new adventure.

My bubble burst the first day when I was placed on a different team without my friends! I couldn't believe it. My team was sent to a rural area where I had to hike up the mountains to tiny villages. The villagers hauled their daily water from tiny watering holes. That meant no running water, no flushing toilets, and no electricity. I was shocked when I realized we had to use holes in dirt floors as bathrooms! My friends were sent in vans to schools in the inner cities; my experience was very different from theirs.

In hindsight, I wouldn't change anything about this mission trip—not even the fact that I was separated from my "besties." It didn't take long before everyone on my team was my friend. We learned to depend on each other for support, and we worked side by side. Our goal was to perform skits and sing songs that brought the Bible alive for these villagers. The trip was crazy, and the experience unforgettable.

In Guatemala Tanja and her friends were considered different due to their fair skin and blonde hair. People would chase after them and ask for autographs to be written in their copies of *Book of Hope*. Wayne and I knew the experience of seeing a different culture would open our daughter's eyes to the broader world. Tanja's next mission trip was to an orphanage in Poland. There, she and her friends fit in; blond hair and blue eyes were the norm.

Tanja Speaks

In Poland we stayed in one place. We ran a summer camp for an orphanage. Poland was more of an eye-opening experience for me even though Guatemala was a poverty- stricken country. Spending 10 days with the same group of children and being able to really impact and change their lives is something I've never forgotten. I'm in contact even now with people from the orphanage who found me on Facebook. We made real connections there.

These experiences helped shape Tanja's empathetic temperament and soft heart for people. Today, she and her husband, Marc, serve in a small-town church plant. Tanja works with the children while Marc runs the soundboard for the service. Together they're raising their children to love the Lord God.

Victoria's journey in youth group was unexpectedly difficult. Issues began as early as kindergarten when she attended our neighborhood school. Victoria was old enough to join the Missionettes at our church—a children's organization similar to the Girls Scouts. At the time, I taught first grade in our church school, and the girls from my classroom took Victoria into their circle. She thoroughly loved having these girls as her friends. However, when I left the church school a year later to teach elsewhere, Victoria was ostracized. After that experience she shied away from making friends at our church. Years later, that same group of girls were in her church youth group, but Victoria was unable to penetrate the strong clique that had developed among the girls in her age group. So Victoria chose to hang out with Tanja's age group.

Throughout her high school years, Victoria continued to build a shell around herself that further alienated her socially, both at school and church. Her teen years were uncomfortable and often painful. Thankfully, as an adult, she can stand and testify about how God is able to break through all barriers as she finds her strength in Him.

Chapter 7

Mom Goes Back to School

In the midst of raising our brood, I made the hair-raising decision to go back to school for a teaching degree. The walls of our small house were starting to close in on me. Friction was growing within the small, shared spaces between my day care children and our older children. By necessity, all the rooms in our downstairs had to be multi-use space. It had also become apparent to me that I did care a bit more about money than my childhood prayer indicated. I realized that a career change would increase our financial stability significantly, and since I couldn't imagine a career that didn't involve children, teaching called to me. Therefore, it was time to close the doors of my home day care and embrace a new aspiration.

Some people might find it difficult or even painful to be the older woman sitting in a college classroom. However, after I recovered from my initial terrified reaction, it became an oasis of tranquility. At my core, I am a forever-student. I have an innate passion for learning and an unquenchable thirst to be in the pages of a book.

As with many of my favorite books, the next chapter of my life was a real page-turner. Once I held that teaching certificate in my hands, I got the idealistic notion that I had to find the perfect school—one that had the perfect classroom just for me. My first classroom was an after-care position in a town that offered only half-day kindergarten. That position was akin to day care, only a stepping-stone toward teaching in a regular elementary school classroom. Next, I spent two years as a first-grade teacher in our church school. Although I cared deeply about this school's mission, my paycheck was smaller than my day care income. I have always believed that God has a sovereign plan instead of life being a random sequence of events, and these early teaching positions helped me to grow in resilience, patience, and knowledge.

From these "not-perfect" positions, I began to see the importance of working with a strong, supportive teaching team. I started to understand my own strengths and weaknesses, and I learned that the classroom would be my teacher. Best of all, I learned to pay closer attention to God's voice. His plan is perfect, but I will never be perfect. And I realized that I don't have to be perfect. What a relief!

In Search of My Dream Teaching Job

Every good story has a climax. The point of high tension came for me in September 2000. I was in prayer again, looking for the school that would be mine. I heard there was a brand-new elementary school opening in a town next door. They were holding open interviews. The ad said, "Just come with your resume in hand, and you are guaranteed an interview." I wasn't letting this opportunity pass without at least giving it a shot, so I prepared my application and headed for the interview.

I couldn't see the school as I drove down the street. A warning sign on the side of the road alerted drivers that children could be crossing the road, and the brightly painted crosswalk pointed in the direction of a long driveway. I turned and drove up to a sprawling new school. Butterflies filled my stomach as I had that "gut feeling" that this was the school for me. A large brick building with a slanted multi-leveled roof sprawled behind flower beds, and large windows covered the expanse of the front walls. I could almost hear the "Hallelujah" chorus playing in my head.

Suddenly, the butterflies turned into gnats: The long line started at the door, continued down the side of the building, and snaked to the other end of the building. Standing in the line were young teachers looking very polished and pristine. In their hands they carried binders or leather portfolios. Panic set in. Who did I think I was that I would be chosen out of this assortment of brand-new, capable-looking, teachers? My faith took a hike, and I was flooded with doubt. I noticed that an official-looking man was standing next to a bin in front of the school. I decided that the least I could do was ask about the process and the time frame. With heavy legs I ambled over to him. He informed me that I could stand in line for possibly a couple of hours or leave my resume in the bin. Someone would surely look at it later. Defeated, I left it in the bin and walked away.

A few weeks later, I responded to a posted position in the oldest public elementary school in that same town. I was beyond thrilled to be called in for an interview. The interview team consisted of teachers and administrators who were in my age bracket. They quickly put me at ease. As the questions flowed, my nervousness fled, which in itself was a huge answer to prayer. I left feeling that the interview had been a success, which was confirmed when they called me back for a demo lesson.

I had been chosen! I was over the moon and jumping for joy. The icing on the cake was that the demo lesson was with preschool children. For the demo requirement I had to plan and execute a lesson with students. This included writing up the lesson with objectives and a detailed plan. Preschool is the group I felt most confident with. During the demo lesson, I chose to ignore the interview team and enjoy the kids, and that turned out to be the best choice I could have made.

Finally, the call I had been waiting for came. I got the job. We had such a wonderful conversation going until I learned that the position was for a part-time kindergarten teacher. I clearly heard a soft voice in my spirit whisper, *"Take it."* Instead, I refused the offer. We needed my full-time paycheck and the insurance that came along with it.

A few days later, this same voice whispered a strong *no* as I accepted a full-time teaching position in a charter school. Shaking off my misgivings, I decided to spend a day getting to know my classroom. I had a lot to do. School was starting in just a few weeks. The secretary showed me to my classroom and left. I wandered aimlessly around the room. I pictured opening day. But, in my mind's eye, I couldn't see the boards all decked out for learning with little people sitting at their desks, and I couldn't see myself in that classroom. A plan wouldn't come into focus. The sinking, sick feeling that I had made the wrong decision took up full residence in my heart and mind. I went home discouraged and scared.

You're probably shaking your head right now saying, "Why doesn't she learn?" I've often wondered why I can be so thick-headed. My faith was at an all-time low. I hung my head and called out to God. Proverbs 3:5 instructs me to trust in the Lord; however, I had failed to trust in the Lord with all my heart. Instead I was leaning on my own understanding of our financial situation and not on his ability to provide for us.

God Provides the Perfect Teaching Position

The climax of a story is not complete until the story turns toward the solution, and God had the solution ready. The next week I received another call from the public school where I had turned down the part-time kindergarten class teaching position. This time, they offered me a full-time first-grade classroom. They didn't just offer the position but insisted they wouldn't take no for an answer. The next week when I walked into this first-grade classroom, my mind's eye was working just fine. I walked around planning, building bulletin boards, and arranging and rearranging tables and chairs with a master plan coming into clear focus.

Let this experience give you a word of encouragement. God wants to live in our personal, private space with us. He desires an intimate relationship with you and me. He is constantly talking to us. But in order to hear him, we need to be still. First Samuel 12:16 tells us to *"stand still and see this great thing the Lord is about to do before your eyes!"* Look for his possibilities and hear his voice speaking into your heart. Don't hesitate to be obedient and to act upon what you hear. I've learned that it is always in my best interest to have God in my corner, and I'm growing in my listening and obedience skills. Finally!

I love it when a writer wraps up a story with a great epilogue. So here goes: Two years later, God wrapped up this chapter in my life with an unexpected gift. I loved the school I was in, but it was only a kindergarten-through-first-grade school. I had always hoped to teach every grade within my professional license. That meant eventually I would need to teach in a school that went up to third grade. In the spring of my second year, the principal announced that two first-grade classes would be removed from our building and relocated to the brand-new school that I had walked away from two years prior. And yes, my class was chosen to be one of those first-grade classes.

I have since taught every grade level under my license and have settled into third grade. To this day as I drive into the school parking lot, I thank God for his plan and purpose in my life. Jeremiah 29:11 tells me that his plans are always to give me hope and a future. I have learned that I can trust in him. He's got me!

Chapter 8

Beginning of Turbulence and Tragedy

The added bonus of marrying into a family of nine siblings, in addition to having my small nuclear family, was the multiplication factor of cousins. Each of our children had several cousins their own age. Super strong bonds developed across our extended families, intertwining into each other's lives and providing a large network of support. Many of Victoria's positive memories stem from sweet times spent with extended family.

Victoria Speaks

There was never a dull moment growing up in our home. To say we had a full house would be an understatement. I was the youngest of the crew, but I was never left out. I was the constant but welcome tagalong. As a result, I became close with all my siblings' friends. My brothers' friends were all like big brothers to me, always looking out for me and being protective. Everyone who lived with us over the years was an extension of my family. I loved having a big family. My two counterpart cousins and I were inseparable for most of our childhood. Every weekend we would rotate between each other's homes. These were some of the best memories of my life.

I praised God for the unity and love within our families. Surprisingly, this great strength ultimately became a weakness for some. The children grew up together, played together, and eventually, some fell together.

Hard Ground

Over those turbulent teenage years, going to church was not a matter of choice for our household. It was a regular habit, which possibly lulled me into believing that my kids were safe from the evils of the world. However, we began to notice signs that our tribe was not immune to the usual temptations and choices of the culture surrounding them. Evidence mounted when kids began to experiment with alcohol, chewing tobacco, and pot.

By the time Corey and Timmy were in their late teens, the third floor was fully occupied by a multitude of boys, and their favorite pastime was watching sports together. From one of Timmy's closest friends, we learned that drinking during the games became a regular activity; it began innocently with just a few beers. Initially, their focus was to have fun, which meant parties and at times drinking until they passed out. Of course, in my world where wrong and right matter, this was something to worry about. I knew the statistics of alcoholism, and I had always held high expectations of abstinence for my kids.

Shockingly, Kevin, one of the teens in this close-knit group, became the first tragic statistic. After an all-night drinking party, he decided to make a breakfast run to McDonalds. In that fateful predawn hour, still under the influence of alcohol, he crashed his car. He lost his life and also took the life of the 15-year-old girl who accompanied him.

This tragedy affected the whole gang who had grown up together. It shook everyone up and served as a wake-up call for some. Thankfully, some kids used Kevin's untimely death to put the brakes on their drinking. Sorrow-filled tears were shed by all, and Face Book pages exploded with childhood memories and many epitaphs. However, the result was both positive and negative. Instead of pulling some of the kids away from drugs and alcohol, this tragedy pulled some in deeper.

The Battle with Addiction Begins

Between the ages of 19 and 22, alcohol took a deep hold of Timmy. It became his anesthetic for physical and emotional pain. It became his social crutch. He could overcome his quiet persona with a few drinks, becoming the life of the party. Victoria followed a similar path but at a much younger age. Her drinking began in her early teens.

I had to question whether we had given our children too much freedom. Should we have been stricter parents? In our home the job of primary caregiver for the children mainly fell on my shoulders. I was home full time during the kids' early years while Wayne worked six days a week. Often his day started at dawn, and he didn't walk back in the door until after the kids' bedtime.

When I became a teacher, the beauty of a teaching schedule was the vacations and the end-of-day school bell. Raising children, doing homework, and holding teacher-parent conferences all fell on my to-do list, while car and home maintenance fell on Wayne's to-do list. I've always appreciated that the cooking, laundry, and grocery shopping fell to both of us. I believe what I've just described are typical family roles for our generation.

I felt it was my job to keep a close eye on our children, so self-recrimination and blame became a nagging whip in my hand. I used it often against myself when things started going wrong for two of our children. It was my job as a mom to teach my kids how to live safe and healthy lives. I had failed miserably. Did you notice all my "I" statements? Perhaps you're a little like me. Foolishly, I thought I was in charge of our home and of our children. And, perhaps, I was in many instances. Just not in all.

Learning to Discern God's Faithfulness

On the journey through addiction, I found myself tested beyond my strength. I also learned something very beautiful and wonderful: When my strength fails, the Lord's is sufficient. When I can no longer endure the pain, his peace is abundant. When I have no more words to pray, the Holy Spirit will put a song in my heart. With the testing, he will also provide a way out so that I may be able to endure it.

Through some very painful years, we watched as occasional, social drinking turned into drug addiction for two of our children. The slide was slow and insidious. It took us by surprise, but through it all, the Lord proved himself faithful.

Chapter 9

Decline into Dark Days – Cycles of Pain and Denial

During Timmy's school years, he showed an exceptional aptitude for art. He amazed us and his art teachers with a skill that showed such promise. Many years later, his very lifelike painting of a deer still hangs in my hallway. In the early days, Timmy was also the one who enforced my house rules in the teen quarters. He laid down the law when friends stepped over the line. He was also the first one to jump in and support friends going through difficult situations.

School is often a traumatic time and place: Friendships are often built and broken at a rapid rate. Beginning in elementary school, both Timmy and Victoria would find that "best friend" who meant so much, only to have him or her move away, be placed in another classroom, or choose someone else for a best friend. This cycle continued, and they both built protective walls around their tender hearts.

Teenage years are a time when emotions are strong and intense.

In Timmy's high school years, we started to see increasing depression and anxiety creep into his life. He couldn't see the beauty in his artwork or find peace in his days. He began to sabotage many of his friendships, not allowing anyone close. Drinking just a few beers for fun quickly escalated into a problem. All signs pointed to Timmy struggling to control his alcohol consumption.

We pushed for Timmy to seek counseling. We realized he needed to see someone for his depression and anxiety; however, in his eyes, only "crazy" people went to a counselor. He wouldn't broach the topic or take any steps to find help. It was difficult for me to sit back and allow him to refuse treatment. I was used to making medical appointments for the kids when they were young, but my hands were tied. Timmy was too old for me to force into a doctor's office. I want to go on record saying that there are many good reasons to seek out a counselor or mental health care provider. Getting the right kind of help could save your loved one's life. It could save your life.

One fateful night Timmy crashed his brand-new motorcycle while driving drunk. This tragic accident altered the course of his life. That cataclysmic night was the beginning of a series of events that no one would have foreseen ending so disastrously. The first domino to fall in the series was our long-awaited 25th wedding anniversary cruise.

We had planned and paid in advance, so we could thoroughly enjoy our first-ever cruise together. The fun was tripled with our traveling companions: my sister and her husband who share our anniversary and my cousin and her husband who live in Finland. We flew to Florida, and from there boarded a huge cruise ship. As the ship pulled away from the dock, we all joined the excited crowd on deck waving goodbye to no one in particular.

Meanwhile at home, the second domino was about to fall. When the parents are away, the children left at home will play. Tearfully, Tanja claims that what happened next was all her fault.

Tanja Speaks

Sometimes when you parents would go out of town, we children would decide to throw a party at your house. I always cleaned up really good so that you wouldn't be the wiser. I threw the party that night. All my friends from my class came. The guys from the basketball team came. Timmy was at the party, but Corey hibernated up in his apartment. He never joined our parties.

Late into the night, someone had the brilliant idea that we should go play basketball at Rocketland. Because the courts stayed lit all night, this was often one of our middle-of-the-night adventures. So, after partying all evening, we all drove to the courts. rode, and The night continued with shooting hoops and having fun running around being stupid kids on a basketball court.

When it was time to leave, I begged Timmy to let me ride home with him because I hadn't had a chance to ride with him on his new motorcycle. He thought about it and almost said yes. But he changed his mind because he only had one helmet. Thank God he changed his mind, because I would have been injured or possibly worse. I would have been on that bike without a helmet.

The motorcycles left the basketball court in advance of the cars. By the time the cars made it partway home, the rider who had been with Timmy met the group with news of his accident.

Not more than a half mile from our house, Timmy's motorcycle was sprawled in the street. He lay among the debris strewn around the road. Timmy was so drunk that he eventually got up yelling at the first responders that he was OK, and that he could walk home. He had suffered severe skin abrasions, and his left arm dangled—clearly out of the shoulder socket. The first responders coerced him into the ambulance.

There's more to this tale—one more domino to be exposed. Timmy had a very specific reason for being at this party, and that is why Tanja felt she was to blame for Timmy's accident.

Tanja Speaks

Whenever I would throw a party when you guys were gone, Timmy was always there. He was there to protect us and make sure the boys would behave themselves. I was the party thrower. I was the social butterfly. I didn't supply the alcohol, but kids brought the alcohol with them. We played games and had a great time. As soon as Timmy knew you guys had left the house, he came home. He would make sure he stayed up until the last person was gone. He wasn't at the party to "party." He wouldn't let us go to Rocketland that night alone with the group of boys.

Tim was always our protector no matter where we were or what we were doing. His drinking was a social lubricant because he was not a social person. Being at a party was hard for him. We even tried to keep the party a secret because we thought he would ruin

things. My big brother was always watching! He was
always looking out for us. I was never the big drinker,
but I loved the social aspect of a party. He always
showed up and scared the boys away. But even though
we tried to hide our parties, he always found out.

This accident caused a lifelong injury to Timmy's shoulder. He suffered chronic, debilitating pain in his shoulder and permanent loss of motion in his left arm. Visits to doctors were to no avail. His job working for Wayne's hardwood floor company over the ensuing years was physically taxing, and chronic pain was his daily companion. The pain was one excuse that allowed him to self-medicate. I don't believe it was the only factor.

Eventually, alcohol and pain prescriptions weren't enough, and Timmy spiraled into heroin addiction. His self-hatred mushroomed and became an all-consuming thought pattern in his life. During these years, the signs of substance abuse were apparent. However, it was also extremely difficult for me to believe and face the situation. Timmy stopped looking me in the eye during our conversations. He was distant and on an emotional rollercoaster of highs and lows. He sat on the couch in a daze staring vacantly at the TV and nodding off. I prayed. Then I prayed even harder. When we smelled the smoke of candles from his room, I wondered, but was afraid to ask, *why was he lighting candles?*

I found it difficult to force myself to face this scary and uncomfortable situation. Our conversations became increasingly confrontational. Confrontations have always made me uncomfortable, and I've spent a lifetime trying to avoid them. Over time, it became easier to ignore the problem facing us than to continue provoking arguments. Wayne and I couldn't seem to make any headway. When money started disappearing from Wayne's company account, we had to face the fact that we had to act.

In those early years of this battle, we watched the son we loved morph into someone else. His dreams for himself as well as our dreams for him were crashing. Our fears continually grew. Grief and sorrow warred with denial as we attempted to save him. We had been living in a paralyzed state, unable to address what was going on with Timmy.

Timmy ran his own crew for the floor company, and Wayne depended on him at work. Along with Corey, Timmy had become invaluable and extremely talented in creating beautiful hardwood floors. Yet, I couldn't get beyond thinking, "*There's no way Timmy would do drugs; he's just drinking again. This happens to other people. It couldn't be happening to us.*"

Chapter 10

Corey's Quest Fuels Him

P erhaps you're wondering: "Well, what about Corey? How was he doing? How was he resisting the pull of the party scene?" His words say it best, so I'll let him answer for himself.

Corey Speaks

Since my early gymnastics days and throughout my teen years, I wouldn't do anything that would diminish my goals and make me weaker. I always had an important question to answer. Nothing could tear my focus from that question.

As a young boy, gymnastics was the funnest thing that I had ever done. I remember doing flips and tricks in the backyard. I thought I was making them all up. I was awestruck when I discovered that gymnastics was a real thing. I could learn from people, and I could do it better. When I realized what the end result could be,

I was very excited. I learned about the different levels that I could possibly attain. I always asked myself, "Is it possible for me to do the next trick? Could I ever be at the level of an elite athlete? Do I have it in me?" I pursued the answers to these questions in the gym.

As a little kid, I didn't know that everyone's body is designed differently. I couldn't understand why I struggled with pommel horse so much. The gymnast supports his weight on his hands holding the pommels, like bars, and moves with his trunk swinging his legs in circles or scissors without stopping.

As an adult, I finally realized that my torso is too long compared to my arms. I have short legs. Whenever I tried to do pommel horse, I couldn't get the right type of elevation to get around the horse. I practiced and trained hours upon hours. I always thought I could overcome anything through willpower. I attained the elite level in all other skills, except with the pommel horse. I was strong in tumbling, rings, and high bar.

At about the age of 12, I finally reached the answer to my questions. I could master the tricks and become an elite gymnast. Once I mentally realized that I could achieve the elite level in gymnastics, the challenge became boring and unfulfilling. I needed a new question to pursue.

I found something much harder than gymnastics. Skateboarding became the new obsession of my life. I figured out early on that skateboarding is much harder than gymnastics. At least for me. Then I was faced with a new question: "Could I become a professional skateboarder?" Only skateboarding mattered, and everything else became irrelevant.

I had one goal in my life: "Am I good enough? Can I achieve professional skateboarding status?" From age 12 to 18, I dedicated myself to pursuing the answer to that question. I always thought that anything could be overcome with willpower. Through some success and many failures, I learned the answer was no. I wasn't good enough.

Skateboarding taught me that I can't overcome everything. Sometimes, I'm just not good enough. No matter what I do. My physical and mental abilities are not good enough, and never could be. It was a hard realization to tell myself I had to move on. It was hard to grapple with.

Timmy was good enough. He could have been a professional skateboarder. He was that much better than me. Timmy didn't put the same internal pressure on himself to achieve a goal as I did. Timmy had the ability but not the drive. He didn't feel the need to take things seriously and into the professional realm. Skateboarding didn't become his life's passion. Instead, he just enjoyed skateboarding. I tried to overcome failure day in and day out but never succeeded, while Timmy handled his board effortlessly. Watching Timmy skateboard was like watching a masterpiece. He could float like an angel while I was a blubbering troll clunking around. I couldn't figure out what the difference was.

Why does one person have that natural ability while another person doesn't? I realized that the trait I was looking for is called finesse. And it carries through everything you do in your life. Timmy had finesse. What also coincides with finesse? Artistic ability. I had the willpower and the drive, but not the finesse or the artistic ability. He had the finesse and the artistic ability that showed up in his skateboarding, his drawings, and later, translated into his work with hardwood floors. I have yet to see anyone else demonstrate the high level of finesse that Timmy owned.

After I figured out I could never become a professional skateboarder at about age 16, I transitioned into powerlifting and bodybuilding, closely followed by mixed martial arts (MMA) fighting. Eventually, I even earned a doctorate degree. I was always in pursuit of answers to these important questions: "Am I capable? Can I attain my next goal?" Focus on my questions overrode the draw of other pursuits that were going on around me. I lived for the conquest. I loved the challenge.

God truly makes each and every one of us unique. There is no one like you or me in this world. I have been blessed with four unique children—each with their own strengths, talents, weaknesses, and challenges. Mercifully, they share the same heavenly Father.

Chapter 11

Standing on the Promises of God

The most amazing moments of my life have been when I held one of my newborn babies in my arms after the work of laboring to bring him or her into this world. My babies were the most beautiful babies. I know every mom feels this way, but mine truly were "perfect."

God's gifts in the form of these little bodies were precious to me. Jeremiah 1:5 tells me that God knew each of my children before he created him or her in my womb. And before they were even born, he sanctified them. This is a wonderful promise from God to me, his daughter. The basic definition of being sanctified is to be set apart for God's use and special purpose. Standing on the promises of God is all I could do as we fought the battle against the evil of heroin addiction in our family.

Standing implies that I am not moving. I am not wavering. While standing on God's promises, I had to plant my mind in God's Word. I can trust that he has my life and my children's lives in his control. What are his promises to you and me as we go through trials? Many of those promises are my favorite verses in the Psalms. I have taken the liberty of paraphrasing some of my favorite promises below:

- **Promise 1:** When I cry out to the Lord, he will hear me. He will deliver our family from the trouble that has overtaken us. Even as our hearts break, he will stay with us, never leaving us. We may have many trials, but he promises to deliver us from them all. (Psalm 34:17–19)
- **Promise 2:** The Lord is my refuge when I am oppressed, my stronghold in times of trouble. I know your name Lord, and I can trust in you. For you Lord, never forsake those who seek you. (Psalm 9:10)
- **Promise 3:** As I take refuge in him, I can be glad. I can sing for joy as he spreads his protection over me. Because I love his name I can rejoice in him. For surely, the Lord blesses the righteous and surrounds them with his favor as a shield. (Psalm 5:11–12)
- **Promise 4:** Because I believe in the Lord Jesus, I will be saved along with my whole family. (Acts 16:29)
- **Promise 5:** God so loved me and my family (and you and your family) that he gave his one and only son, that as we believe on him, we will not perish but have eternal life. (John 3:16)

As we walk into terrible storms, God comes alongside us. He carries us and loves us. Praying scripture was, and is, a great source of hope. We can stand strong on the promises of God through heartache and fear.

I think that expressing my love to each of my children was something I took for granted. It was so easy to hug and cuddle them when they were babies and preschoolers. But as they got older, it seemed harder to demonstrate the love that was in my heart. In hindsight, I realize that the most challenging and important thing I could have done was to show Timmy or Corey or Tanja or Victoria how much I loved each one of them unconditionally. I think our love as parents becomes unconditional when we realize that no matter what our children do, we still love them.

Children go through that awkward stage where they push parents away from a hug. Definitely, a kiss is taboo! By the time my kids reached their teen years, I had settled into acting out of my Finnish heritage, which tended to be somber and unemotional. I was raised by parents who showed little affection or emotion. In my home, it was *understood* that my sister and I were loved; my parents assumed that didn't need to be spoken. I've tried to break that pattern over the years of raising my children, but old habits die slowly.

Often, I've heard the question: *"If I could go back in time, what would I change?"* That's an easy question for me to answer. I would gently cradle each of my children's faces, look them in the eye, and say, *"I love you. You are precious to me."* I wish I could teleport back in time and do this for every day that I didn't. I would do it even for the days when I was angry at their choices or disappointed in their actions or proud of their achievements or for no special reason at all.

When our children choose to do the unthinkable, we find that we love them even more. If we earthly parents can love our children through thick and thin, then how much more can we believe that our heavenly Father loves them? One of my favorites prayers comes from Jeremiah 29:11: *"For I know the plans I have for you,"* declares the LORD, *"plans to prosper you and not to harm you, plans to give you hope and a future."*

Chapter 12

Another Challenge – Victoria Comes of Age

During our struggles with Timmy, we were involved with a juggling act with Victoria. She was 17 and testing out her wings. She had a job in a clothing store, and she was looking into colleges. Things were looking good. However, we really weren't sure who she was hanging out with or where she was spending her time. She always had an acceptable answer when I asked, but things just weren't sitting right with us.

It's tough to let go as a parent and trust that your child is making the right choices. Before her 18th birthday, she began living her life elsewhere while her belongings and animals stayed behind at our house.

We finally learned she had a boyfriend who was several years older and lived in his own apartment. We discovered that was where she was spending most of her time, days and nights. Soon after Victoria's 18th birthday, she called and set up a dinner date with us, so we could meet this secret boyfriend. My blood pressure skyrocketed through the roof as we talked. *"Why this secrecy? Who was this guy?"* Anxiety and apprehension clouded my thoughts during the drive to the restaurant. *"Why had she chosen to hide this boyfriend? Were we the last to know about him?"*

The waitress escorted us to the table, and Victoria introduced us to the man she was basically living with. He definitely didn't fit the category of a boy. He was a man. I have never had such a strong reaction to a human being as I did to this man. During our meal, I actually pictured myself jumping over the table and choking him to death! Everything in me coiled against him. I felt like every word he said was evil spewing out of his mouth. I clutched the bench seat with both hands, afraid I would actually follow through on my thoughts. Through the conversation it became clear that he was not the man God would have provided for our daughter. Both Wayne and I worked hard to act civil and not further alienate our daughter from us.

When we walked out of the restaurant, I wanted nothing more than to grab hold of Victoria and drag her out with us. But it was clear that she had made her decision to stay with him.

Our next step was to investigate this man through any channels open to us. We questioned siblings, cousins, and even called on a family member to connect us with a police investigator. Our research brought to light that this man was known to the police as a dangerous drug dealer. We were told that our daughter was in harm's way and that the police had an active investigation open on him. Upon one of Victoria's visits home, we confronted her with this information. The discussion did not go well. She was furious with us for our interference.

As a result of our action, we saw less of Victoria. When our children are under a threat, a parent's first reaction is to save them. I wanted to solve this problem. I texted her often trying to mend fences. I called every person who I thought could influence her. We racked our brains for a plan, but this boyfriend had been very smart. He knew we didn't have any recourse legally because Victoria was 18. She was an adult, free to make her own choices.

We learned they had been together for almost two years. Our stubborn minds refused to concede that Victoria had chosen such a destructive and scary relationship. How was it possible that she didn't have a problem with his lifestyle? His career? Two burning questions kept haunting me: "*How could she be clean if she was living with a career drug dealer? How could we not have known?*"

Victoria Speaks

It was the morning of his court case in which he was accused of beating up his ex-girlfriend. He and I were both confident it would go in his favor, and he would ultimately prove his innocence. The story that he told me was that his vengeful ex-girlfriend's abusive, alcoholic father had brutally attacked her. But then she'd recanted that claim and had wrongfully blamed it on him. I had no reason not to believe him, especially since his best friend and his brother were willing to testify that they were with him on the night in question.

According to them, the girl came over claiming she had been attacked, and they had only seen the aftermath. Then, my boyfriend and his brother brought her to the hospital.

The court case was thrown out because the ex-girlfriend changed her story once again, saying that my boyfriend was innocent. I was happy it was over but felt in my gut that something was not right. After prying more information out of him and catching him in discrepancies, the truth finally came out. He had caused her injuries, which included a broken nose and knocked-out teeth.

I was unnerved most of all that he had the power to get his victim to retract her accusation and have two witnesses lie on his behalf. I knew I was in way over my head, and I was not sure how I was going to get out. I asked him whether he would do the same to me if I ever made him angry. His answer was no because there were two types of women—the ones that can be reasoned with and ones that cannot. I took that as a warning; as long as I listened and obeyed, I would not meet the same fate as the women before me.

Looking back, I could see God's protection over me. Over the years and thousands of fights, he never did put his hands on me. Even though he wanted to cross that line, it felt as if there were an invisible barrier preventing him. However, he found other ways of keeping me in line. Mostly he would use verbal threats against my family.

Eventually, he started selling Percocet to my brother and other people I knew. Getting close to my brother was just another way to control me. He would allow my brother to have an outstanding bill of thousands of dollars. If I acted out of line, he would harass him to pay immediately, threatening Timmy until I begged him to stop.

He also found my weakness, my love for animals. One morning, after I had left him and moved back home, he called to say something was wrong with his new puppy. He needed to bring it to Tufts Animal hospital. I sped over to his apartment to find a small puppy that could still fit in the palm of my hand. It was struggling to breath.

I could barely contain my anger on the ride to the animal hospital. I knew he was responsible, even though he claimed it was an accident. This was not the first time he had used this tactic to hurt me. My cat Leo that he gave me was staying at my parents' house because after a particularly bad fight, he had "accidentally" stepped on him, fracturing his back leg.

Halfway to the hospital I exploded and started screaming at him. He pulled the car over, grabbed the puppy by the neck and shook it violently. Then he threw the limp puppy back on my lap. It was dead. He turned the car around, and, on the ride back, I sobbed while he unleashed threats as to what would happen if I were to tell anyone. I was so disgusted and horrified. I wanted out, no matter the consequences, but his threats had escalated. He vowed to kill me or my family and said he would happily spend the rest of his life in prison for it.

A few days later he informed me that he had gotten a new pet dog, and I knew what that meant. I agreed to come back if he would give the dog away to a new home.

Chapter 13

Finding Strength in the Waiting Times

W hat do we do when we've exhausted all options? We wait. A search of the King James Version of the Bible, shows that the words *wait* and *waited* are used 141 times. We are encouraged to stay strong and know that our hope is in God. We learn that he will hear us. Psalm 56:8 assures me that he keeps track of all my sorrows. He has collected all my tears in his bottle and recorded each one in his book. That's a whole lot of tears. In the waiting, I have a choice to either grow in faith or despair.

I have chosen to commit each moment of both my good and bad days to Him. Our family was caught in a wild game of ping pong between Timmy's and Victoria's drug addiction dramas.

Confronting Timmy's Addiction with Tough Love

During one of Timmy's disappearing acts, I apprehensively walked to his second-floor bedroom. I was appalled and enraged at what I found. The floor was covered with empty alcohol containers; there were enough bottles to fill at least three recycle bins. Bottles were in and under the bed, in bureau drawers, on the night table—absolutely everywhere I looked. I couldn't believe he would do this in our home. I was shocked at the extent of his problem. I broke down sobbing.

Not only did I find the alcohol bottles, but that afternoon I had a crash course on drug paraphernalia. As I stood looking around the room, my tears turned into hot anger. I made the decision that I wasn't putting up with this any longer. This was *our* house and *our* rules. I spent the next several hours throwing his clothes into trash bags, and all the bags went out on the back porch. I resolved that if he didn't pick them up in two weeks, I would throw them away.

That day I emptied his room completely. Only furniture was left when I was done. I even stripped all the bedding and threw it on the back porch with the clothes.

Next, I called Wayne to let him know Timmy wasn't welcome back home without some serious rehab. He had to go into a program or find somewhere else to live. We were going into tough love mode. When my anger subsided, anguish took its place: *"Had I made the right decision?"* Any parent who's had to show tough love knows how much it hurts. I beat myself up day and night. The nagging question remained: *"Where was Timmy? Was he OK?"*

Eventually, we realized he was climbing in through the cellar window during the day when we were all gone. He was most likely eating from our fridge. Sweet relief and deep sadness filled my heart. I wondered what he thought the first time he went up to his room. My anguish only intensified. I was horrified that I must have really hurt him when he saw what I had done. Did he cry like I had when he surveyed the empty room? Did his heart break to see that his mother had thrown him out? Drug addiction isn't just a cycle for the addict; it's a cycle of tears, fear, and anger for the whole family.

Confronting Victoria's Addiction with Seeds of Hope

We fell into the typical pattern of a family fighting with drug addiction. When Victoria would pop in for visits, she was a whirlwind of contradictions. She would either talk calmly as if life was great or storm out of the house angry, insulted by something I said. I came to rely heavily on Luke 12:12 in which scripture says, *"The Holy Spirit will give you the words to say at the moment when you need them"* (VOICE).

This is one of the best things about being the daughter of the Holy and heavenly Father. He speaks to his children. As I talked to Victoria, another part of my brain talked to God. Often, the words that came from my mouth were a surprise to me. The Holy Spirit speaks words of wise counsel when we allow it. His words bring peace out of strife.

A prominent day etched in my memory was when a strung-out Victoria sat shaking at my kitchen table. She was entering withdrawal symptoms and was unraveling. I walked on eggshells making sure to guard my words and actions. The nagging thought persisted that I should pray over her. Typically, any talk of God would send her into a rage and out the door. That day when I asked to pray, to my greatest surprise, she said, "Yes." I placed both arms on her shoulders and beseeched the Lord over my daughter. She cried and shook through the entire prayer, but she didn't storm out in anger.

With that prayer at the kitchen table, God planted seeds of hope into my heart, and I believe into Victoria's as well.

Victoria Speaks

I'd been fully isolated for a long time, emotionally drained living at my breaking point. I was having panic attacks over the stress of dealing with my boyfriend and still trying to function at school and work. I had done plenty of drugs before and would often take Vicodin to help me sleep but I had never been a huge fan of downers. I preferred alcohol or uppers.

One day my boyfriend crushed up some Percocet and made it into a line. He then handed me the straw. I was hesitant because I saw how hooked other people had gotten on these things but figured I would not let it get that far. I snorted the line and instantly knew I had made a mistake. I didn't just like the feeling, I loved it. After that, the days just faded into weeks and then months. I couldn't go a single day without taking a pill after that first line. Everything changed after that day, and I knew my life would never be the same.

Not only was I different, but he had completely done a 180 in his personality. He claimed he had changed and acknowledged all the wrong he had done over the years. I did not believe him at first, but as time went on, it was like he had transformed into a totally different person.

After an argument, I said I was going to stay at my parents' house for a while. Usually, staying at my parents' house would spark a violent reaction, but he was calm and understanding and said, "Take all the time you need." He could sense my confusion and said, "Go ahead and leave; you will be back at my door begging to be let in."

Determined to prove him wrong, I left. I woke up at five in the morning feeling horrible. I was sick to my *stomach, sweating and shivering at the same time. I called him and told him what was happening. His response was, "Come back, and I'll give you a pill. You'll be fine." When I got to his apartment, he had a line waiting for me. After snorting the line, a wave of relief flooded through my body. Within seconds I felt better than ever.*

That was the moment when I realized why he had changed; he didn't need to get angry anymore since he had complete control over me. My tolerance rapidly increased because there was no limit on how many Percocets I could have. Before long, I was using the street value equivalent to $360 a day. This was not financially sustainable, so as the story goes, with most addicts, the alternative was a cheaper and a more potent option: heroin.

Out of sheer desperation, I began to change how I prayed for Victoria's situation. I started praying specifically for the removal of this boyfriend from her life. I prayed for a permanent removal, and just in case God needed some ideas, I was glad to supply a list:

- Move him to another state or preferably another country. No, that wouldn't do. Victoria would simply go with him.
- He needed to fall for a new girl. No, that would just put someone else in Victoria's shoes.
- A fatal accident would fit the bill. He needed to be dead and buried. I guess I can't pray for that, can I? I did.
- Jail! He needed to go away for many years. Long enough that Victoria would come to her senses.

Time passed, and as it did, unseen things were happening.

Victoria Speaks

My long shift at the bar had just ended. I waited impatiently for my boyfriend to pick me up. When I saw his brother pull up instead, I knew something bad had happened. Soon, I learned that my boyfriend had been shot and placed under arrest at the hospital. Later that night, I opened our apartment door to police officers who promptly put me in handcuffs, stated I was under arrest, and brought me to the police station. During the interrogation, I learned that the charges against him were multiple counts of home invasion and kidnapping. They repeatedly asked me what I knew.

Where is the gun hidden? I honestly didn't know the answer to any of their questions.

As the night wore on, I started withdrawals. The cops waited throughout the night for a search warrant for our apartment to come through. I only cared about one thing: getting to the assortment of pills and drugs that were hidden in my keychain. I had taken them from his stash the moment I found out he was arrested. Unfortunately for me, the cops had taken my keys when I was handcuffed. They promised to return them when they finished with their search. Finally, in the early morning hours, we were back at the apartment. I was left sitting in the cruiser in the driveway, hoping they would not find my stash.

One of the cops strolled over to my window holding up my keys. He complimented my creativity in hiding drugs in the keychain. At this point I knew I looked pathetic. I had been up all night, and I was well into withdrawals. The cop asked whether the drugs were mine, and I didn't have the energy to think up anything better than yes. He stared at me for a while and sighed deeply. Then he told me he had a daughter around my age. He said, throughout the whole night, he had been wondering why someone like me would be caught up with a guy like that.

Then he said, "It's your lucky day." They confiscated the drugs, and I was free to go. I should have felt relieved, but all I could think about was the misery I was going to be in until I could find my next fix.

Eventually, things leveled out and I enjoyed my newfound freedom. My boyfriend was in jail, and a large bail was set. I started using my job as an avenue to get the things I wanted. Being a bartender for so many years, I had perfected a persona that got the most tips out of my regulars. Customers would come and sit for hours listening to me talk about my life, most of which was random stories I made up on the spot with reality and lies blending together. They would have been shocked if they had known that all the money they tipped me was going to feed my drug habit.

But the truth was, deep down, a feeling of being terribly alone continued to grow. I believed all I had were my animals to keep me going. I didn't want to be alive anymore . . . but they needed me.

It wasn't long before I had my eye on a new boyfriend. He was my usual "bad boy" type. He belonged to a motorcycle gang. He also happened to be my boss's son, which definitely turned out to be a conflict of interest.

I felt safe for the first time in a very long time. I knew if my boyfriend got out of jail, he would find it much harder to come after someone who had an entire gang backing them. I immediately moved into my new friend's house. This was my chance to make a change. I went through months of trying to detox myself. I went from relapse to relapse. It was an excruciating process, and my body was so worn out from the abuse. At my lowest, my weight dropped to less than 100 pounds. I felt frail and weak. Eventually, I was able to get clean for a few months, but then turned to drinking to calm the terrible cravings. I got a new bar job and decided to break up with my biker boyfriend and move back home. This was extremely difficult because I was constantly at odds with my family.

Nevertheless, I refused to stay with someone that I didn't love anymore just for a place to live. But going back to my old environment proved to be too much of a trigger. I eventually relapsed and left my parents' house. I was on my own again.

Addiction cut a wide path through our kids' friendship group; no family was left unscathed. It broke our hearts to see so many young people trapped in destructive patterns that involved alcohol and drugs. But our hope is not in the things that we see. Second Corinthians 4:18 tells us to fix our eyes on what is unseen, for what is seen is temporary, but what is unseen is eternal. I can trust my heavenly Father to call my family to him even when I don't see him at work yet.

Chapter 14

Celebrating Family Milestones in the Midst of Struggle

Rays of sunshine broke through the years of struggles as we received wonderful gifts in the births of three precious grandchildren and two beautiful family weddings

Our First Grandchild: Elijah

On what began as a rather ordinary day of the week, Tanja walked into the kitchen and started to talk to me. After her opening line, "Mom I have to tell you something," she burst into tears.

Call it mom's intuition or common sense, but when my 21-year-old daughter has that certain dismal *I'm in trouble* look in her eyes, only one thought comes to my mind. She must be pregnant. Finishing her last year of undergraduate studies was the plan. Looking ahead to beginning her career was the plan. A baby was *not* in the plan. I looked at her and said, "Say it. Say it out loud." Tanja responded with a question. "Do I have to?" And then, finally, through sobs, came the confession: "I'm pregnant."

There were so many possible responses in this situation. My first reaction was anger, followed closely by disappointment. Tanja remembers that she avoided me for a few days. That was probably a wise course of action. It was better for us to take a time-out when both of our emotions were out of control. But over the next week, I remember my excitement growing. *"A baby! How special is that?"* Later that week, I went out shopping for a very important gift. All my children had been blanket babies. They each had their own blanket with silk trim. Each one loved their blanket. I loved their blankets! They would sleep with their blankets every night for years and sometimes drag them outside into the day's adventures. Blankets became tattered and torn and couldn't be washed back to their original color.

Eventually, at a certain age, each child's blanket mysteriously disappeared.

I had to find a blanket for this new baby. I searched one store after another until I finally found the perfect one to give Tanja. With that gift, Tanja knew that her baby was *our* baby. We would be grandparents! I couldn't wait.

Tanja's delivery was long. She labored through the night, and progress was slow. For some reason, the nurse or doctor had neglected to tell us that the baby was turned and facing the wrong way. This was impeding delivery. Finally, it was time for the birth. The monitors had been beeping and humming for hours—until all at once, they stopped. I looked over at the doctor and watched his demeaner change quickly from laid-back to engaged and barking orders. My prayer turned frantic as I repeated the name "Jesus." Finally, we heard the most wonderful sound of a baby wailing.

Then the next most wonderful thing happened: I got to hold the fifth most beautiful baby who had ever been born. Elijah Hunter Hodge entered the world on January 10, 2011. The name Elijah means "the Lord is my God."

"This period of my life was very traumatic," Tanja says. "But I wouldn't change it. I wouldn't take it away. I wouldn't be the person I am today without Elijah." According to Romans 8:28, *"We know that in all things God works for the good of those who love him."* This promise contains a condition. It's contingent on the fact that Tanja loves God. And she does. This love frees up our heavenly Father to work when we follow his leading and when we stray to our own path.

We are all grateful for the most beautiful blessing of this baby boy who was born into our family. Tanja, your dad and I are extremely proud of you. You are a nurturing, strong, and wise Mama.

Our First Wedding: Corey and Kellie

Corey, our elder son, married Kellie on June 24, 2011. Wedding plans ushered in a kaleidoscope of emotions. Hopes and dreams blossomed even as the excitement evoked feelings of nostalgia. Our older son had transformed from a boy into a man. It seemed like just yesterday he was climbing trees and riding bikes.

Now, standing in the bridal boutique, I smiled through tears at Kellie's dress fitting. Never had I seen a more breathtaking bride, and she was wearing the most stunning of gowns. She was a vision of a true princess. Her prince charming was even willing to take dance lessons so their first dance together would be perfect. Weddings open the door to brand-new beginnings in which all things are possible.

Weddings proceed even if the rain clouds cover the sun as they did on that day. What a blessing when the sun peeked out and pushed away the raindrops for their outdoor ceremony. Every bride plans the entrance of the processional in order to ensure the bridal march will run as smoothly as possible. However, the bridal party was hampered as each pair of heels got sucked into the wet ground. Just keeping shoes on became the challenge. Even so, the beautiful wedding transpired perfectly on the elegant lawn of the Glen Manor House. Welcome to our family, Kellie.

At the reception, I had the pleasure of the only mother and son dance I've had with Corey. As the music of Rascal Flats played "My Wish," I held back tears. It seemed hard to believe that Corey was married. That he was an adult! How quickly the years had passed by. As we danced, my heart echoed the chorus while the band played on.

Fast-forward nine years: Corey and Kellie have a beautiful little girl named Liberty Rose. She is full of spunk; her little body seems to be in perpetual motion. As soon as she hears a tune, the budding ballerina within her breaks out in jumps and twirls, with contagious laughter swirling around her. Unlike her Grammy, she's got rhythm! At the age of two, she's a pro at blowing kisses. This petite little firecracker stole our hearts from first sight. Thank you, God, for your extraordinary gift.

Corey Speaks

I have come to the awakening that I do not have to chase the question, "Am I capable of pushing myself to the limit?" It is time to channel my energy into a sustainable goal, which leads to the life I want to live with my family. We are building a new dream together. We envision owning several hundred acres of wooded land. In the middle, encircled by trees, we will build our own house, barns, and sheds. We will grow our gardens and farm our little piece of earth. My new quest is to homestead. I'm following the call, which is leading me to where I'm supposed to be. I am following the path to where life feels right.

I was a city kid who escaped every summer to the cabin in the woods. In the peace and quiet of the forest, I find solace. I am free. With each step into the forest, I leave behind stress and strain and become recharged and energized. Excitement replaces anxiety as I wonder, "What will I find? Is there a 300-pound deer just behind the next tree?" Here is where I feel alive. Here is where I belong.

Blessings Continue: Another Wedding, Another Grandchild

Eight years later, on a beautiful October afternoon, Tanja married Marc, a soft-hearted and kind man. The close-knit family of two became three. A little over a year later, Tanja stood in my kitchen and announced, "Mom, I'm pregnant." This time I was hoping for and anticipating those words. They were an answer to prayer. I could hardly curb the urge to go shopping. I had to find a blanket with the signature silk trim. Thank you, God, for your miracles. Now this small family of three has blossomed into a family of four.

Tanja Speaks

Etched in the recesses of my memory is a picture of my mother studying well into the night. We lived without her on weekends as she progressed through a master's program in education. As a middle school student, I was greatly impressed by her fortitude to change our lives for the better. It was the highlight of my year, as well, to watch her walk across the stage to receive her degree. I resolved right then and there that I would reach that same goal in my life.

I have kept that promise. In May 2017, my family had the honor of sitting in the nosebleed section of the enormous convention center in our city, as I walked across the stage to receive my master's degree. The challenging season of persevering through the combination of work, studies, and being a mom ended with elation.

Together, Marc and I are building a healthy and happy home. We look forward to owning a house in the burbs with room for some country extras. We will try our hand at raising a few chickens and possibly a goat or two. My greenhouse and gardens will flourish with flowers and vegetables. Our children, Elijah and Emilia, will know the joy that God and his gifts provide.

Chapter 15

Time to Find Another Farmhouse

O ver the years, the walls of our Cambridge Street house started to close in even though we had expanded our living space as much as possible. The families who knew our names moved out, and strangers took their places. The noise of summer neighborhood parties and the vehicles on the busy street at all hours of day and night increased as the years rolled by.

One day, huge bulldozers rolled in, and a grocery store emerged across the street. Harsh bright lights from the parking lot glared throughout the night. In our bedroom we could clearly hear the bird-like chirp of the crossing light. Why would someone need to use the crossing light in the dead of night? Why would someone be out walking at two in the morning? Often, the answer was to get to the bar five buildings down across the street. The neighborhood changed dramatically, bar fights spilled into the street during the summer, needles and shot bottles littered the street, and drug interactions became common in the area.

But selling the house and getting out wasn't easy for us. Both Wayne and I had a serious lack of faith that our Cambridge Street house would sell. It still needed quite extensive rehab and obviously, we were not located in the best part of the city.

One week when I was being particularly whiny to God about this matter, Corey popped his head in the door. His visit was unexpected and abrupt. Without so much as a hello, he looked at me and asked, "Why haven't you sold this house and moved?" His tone was angry, so I blustered my excuses, ending with the final one: "I don't know any realtors." He stared me down and replied, "I'll get back to you tomorrow," and he walked back out the door as abruptly as he had walked in. The next day Corey sent me the name and number of a realtor. That stopped my whining cold turkey. Our house sold in two weeks for the asking price!

God had sent Corey to light a fire under me. His God-appointed visit was the catalyst for kicking my inertia to the curb. Ephesians 3:20 tells me to give *"all glory to God, who is able, through his mighty power at work within us, to accomplish infinitely more than we might ask or think"* (NLT). Then God added the icing to the cake. He gave us the "infinitely more" than we dared to ask and took us where our lack of faith wouldn't allow us to go.

He led us to another little old farmhouse. This house, too, was well over 100 years old and had once been surrounded by a countryside filled with pastures. The pastures had been divided into lots, and houses spread over the land. However, this time the city didn't encroach any further. Instead, the neighborhood maintained its green grass, and white daisies covered its hills.

The little farmhouse sat sad and lonely. Her paint was cracked and dirty. She looked shabby, though she was just as good a house as ever underneath. Best of all, her wonderful partner, the big red barn, still stood strong and majestic by her side. We promptly fell in love and became the proud owners of a farmhouse without a farm and a barn without cows. I'm actually really OK without the cows.

We fixed the windows and walls and painted the interior walls a lovely shade of gray. Family and friends toiled beside us for over two years, pulling down walls and ceilings, ripping up floors, and rebuilding them stronger. This house was also a huge rehab special like those on HGTV, and we made it all the way to the "big reveal." God used people in our lives to answer our prayer and meet our need. I am so thankful that I finally obeyed instead of continuing with excuses and whining.

You might be wondering about the "infinitely more" that God gave us. This new house is in the heart of our playground. We have our own private entrance onto the walking and biking trail that I used to drive 15 miles to access. From the "new" farmhouse, I only have to walk out my door and head to my favorite jogging route around the reservoir. We have yet to finish exploring the many hiking and biking paths available to us in the area. God is good, and he loves to give good gifts to his children.

Chapter 16

Endless Cycle of Relapse, Confrontation, Rehab, and Hope

Timmy's roller-coaster ride continued with cycles of relapse, confrontation, rehab, and hope. Each time he returned to "normal" life, he would lose sight of that hope and fall back into relapse. Timothy stood as his own accuser, seeing himself with condemning eyes, judging himself as "unworthy." He wept bitterly many nights as we sat together on the couch urging him into a new rehab program. It was exhausting emotionally and physically for him and us. He was riddled with shame and defeat as he continued on this destructive path.

After completing program after program, Timmy's perspective didn't turn around. Henry Ford is quoted as saying, "If you think you can or you think you can't . . . you're right." Timothy thought he couldn't. His thought pattern set limits on his recovery, on hope, and on God.

Along with encouraging Timmy into rehab programs, we pushed for him to see a therapist. Regrettably, he held onto his preconceived notion that only "crazy" people went to mental health providers. I have to say I believed he fit the category at that point.

A plethora of nagging questions and doubts lodged in my mind: "*Were we too lenient? Had we failed our children? Was the neighborhood in which we raised them partly, or even completely, to blame for the choices Timmy and Victoria had made? Perhaps if we had moved when the kids were young, we wouldn't be fighting this battle.*" But when I surveyed other families who lived in better neighborhoods, many were fighting the same battle. Drugs and alcoholism do not stop at neighborhood boundaries. Addiction doesn't care whether you're rich or poor. Drug addiction is truly unbiased, welcoming all to take part.

Ironically, Romans 7:22–25 is in the scripture rolodex that Timmy gave me. The struggle Paul describes in this passage bears witness to Timmy's anguish:

> *For in my inner being I delight in God's law; but I see another law at work in me, waging war against the law of my mind and making me a prisoner of the law of sin at work within me. What a wretched man I am! Who will rescue me from this body that is subject to death? Thanks be to God, who delivers me through Jesus Christ our Lord! So then, I myself in my mind am a slave to God's law, but in my sinful nature a slave to the law of sin.*

Timothy hated his drug abuse lifestyle, but he continued to cycle back into it even as he fought it in his own strength.

Most people, including myself, would call Wayne and me enablers. However, I could never bring myself to throw Timmy out again or stop calling Victoria. It had hurt too much the first time I emptied Timmy's room. When I came to the end of me, when I could not even pray anymore, when no words were possible, that was when the peace of the Lord was at its greatest in my heart.

We were living in a state of perpetual fear for both Timmy and Victoria. Sleep was a very fleeting thing, as I prayed through the quiet hours between eleven o'clock at night and three in the morning. Those became my prime praying hours. During one of these tearful prayer sessions in the night, the Lord gave me a vision. In it, I saw a side view of Timmy standing with both arms raised in praise and worship. What I saw was, in itself, a vision of a miracle because Timmy couldn't raise his left arm above shoulder height. His arm had remained frozen from his motorcycle accident many years before this vision. His expression in the vision was one of complete surrender and worship.

Some might say it was my overactive imagination or probably just a dream. Others might chalk it up to wishful thinking, but I believe it was an image of hope and a promise from my merciful heavenly Father. This image has never dulled in my memory.

My battle strategy was constant 24/7 prayer. Sometimes, my prayer was as simple as saying the name of Jesus with an upraised hand. Other times, it meant reading scripture substituting specific names in pivotal places. Often prayer was having worship music on so that it filled my thoughts with promising lyrics. Old-time hymns from my childhood would unexpectanly pop into my head and sustain me in dark hours.

I have learned that strength comes from the heart of God. The closer I drew to him the closer he drew to me. Often, when Timmy came out of the programs he would return to work with

Wayne and Corey at our floor company. There were short and long stretches of sobriety. During these times when he looked me in the eye, I saw the soul of my humble and kind son. Again.

Matthew 6:22, tells us, *"The eye is the lamp of the body. If your eyes are healthy, your whole body will be full of light."* I could always tell when either Timmy or Victoria was back on their drug of choice. There would be a physical change in their eyes and faces. Matthew 6:23 continues, *"But if your eyes are unhealthy, your whole body will be full of darkness. If then the light within you is darkness, how great is the darkness!"* Drug addiction is an invading demon of darkness that comes to steal our children's souls.

This demon constantly beckoned Timmy until he would stumble and fall. A trigger would cause him to break down again, and the pattern would continue. Eventually, he couldn't make enough money to support his addiction. Then he would start stealing money from the floor company account and our credit cards. At that point, we had a decision to make. We could press charges and put our son in jail. He had stolen enough for it to be a felony charge. This was an agonizing decision, and we just weren't strong enough to have him charged. Instead, we forced him into yet another program. The cycle continued, and the next time, he was caught and charged with stealing from a Target department store.

One of my lowest moments was seeing Timmy sitting in the courtroom in shackles with his head hanging down. I was sick to my stomach wondering how he or we could possibly get through this. We sat not moving for a long time after his hearing was over, unable to get up. One of the bailiffs finally came over and told us we could leave. I assume he didn't realize we were frozen in place. We had no idea what to do next.

For the second time, Timothy went to Teen Challenge, which is a recovery program with Christ at its core. This time it was court-mandated that he stay for the full term of 15 months. The Lord truly gave us and Timmy a season of rest.

Timothy became my humble and kind son, once again. There was nothing as precious to me as seeing the real Timmy emerge. During a Teen Challenge service, I sat in tears as I listened to my extremely shy son proclaim the Lord in his life in front of a congregation of people. God promises restoration, and that is what we witnessed in Timmy. Grief is not a permanent condition in our lives because our God brings joy out of sorrows. Instead, grief is part of the peaks and valleys of our journey toward home.

Chapter 17

Victoria Breaks out of the Cycle

V ictoria's journey through this destructive lifestyle looked very different than Timmy's. She lived outside our home, while he was a daily fixture in our home. Both isolated themselves and had a very small sphere of friends. Timmy stayed close to family while Victoria jumped from one detrimental male relationship into another. They shared a fear of being vulnerable and an intense insecurity in social situations. Their acts of alienation as a form of self-protection catapulted them into further self-destructive behaviors.

Victoria Speaks

Addiction is a very powerful tool that Satan uses to trap humans. No matter how bad you want to stop and no matter how many clean days you've managed to rack up, you have this ever-looming fear that you'll never make it out alive. Addiction takes everything from you and does not discriminate on whom it victimizes. It doesn't matter what the drug is or who the addict is, the story is the same: a loss of free will and the sacrifice of your mind, body, and soul. I imagine Satan particularly enjoys using addiction because he can toy with his victims before he devours them.

Most heroin addicts describe their initial encounter with the drug as falling in love. This is so common, in fact, that at rehab, they had us write a love letter to our drug of choice and then afterward write a break-up letter. The feeling that drug addicts attribute to their drug of choice just so happens to be the strongest emotion a human being can feel. Love can make a person do crazy and irrational things; it can be an all-consuming emotion. Addicts often end up doing things they would never have imagined—all for the love of the drug.

My own experience with heroin felt like an abusive and controlling relationship. Just like a relationship with a person, you have that initial honeymoon phase where you fall head over heels in love and feel like nothing could go wrong. I would describe the first couple of months as pure happiness. I felt I had found the answer to all my life's problems and the cure to all my pain. I couldn't imagine my life without the drug and never wanted to go a single day apart from it. Most people take opioids to numb physical pain, but in my case, the drug was used to numb emotional pain.

As time went on, the feeling that this was too good to be true started to creep in. I tried to ignore it and make excuses; I tried desperately to drown out my conscience. Despite my efforts, things started to change drastically for the worse, and the relationship began to morph into something ugly.

Like an abusive relationship, the drug demanded complete control and submission. It required my undivided attention; I spent all my energy and time on it. If I attempted to leave, it became physically abusive, throwing my body into violent withdrawals. It slowly stripped me of my dignity and self-worth. It secluded me from all outside relationships, for fear of anyone coming between us. I was trapped, with no one else to blame but myself. Eventually, I lost hope and got tired of fighting and settled into the idea that this was to be the rest of my life.

I was looking for a place to live when one of my regular bar patrons introduced me to his friend who owned real estate properties. Jason was different from the guys I was used to. For starters, he wasn't a "bad boy." His only interest in me was to find me an apartment.

Surprisingly, for once I was interested in someone based on their good qualities rather than their bad-boy side. He was successful and responsible—someone I would not be embarrassed to be seen with. He also liked motorcycles and fast cars, so in my eyes he was the full package, and the best of both worlds. At first, he was all business, helping me look for an apartment, but the more we talked the more our relationship grew. His friend who introduced us had painted a picture of me as the perfect girl, and I tried my best to keep up the charade. I didn't want to scare him away. We talked often, and soon our relationship matured into more than a friendship. But the person he had been told I was, did not exist. We were already falling in love, and it was amazing. Then he asked me to move in. I felt sick. Knowing that I was living a lie, I needed to tell him the truth but could never seem to get it out. I had him completely snowed.

After quite some time, I decided I had to set the record straight. We were going out to a fancy restaurant, and I decided that was the night to tell him the truth. I just needed to get it over with. Sitting across the table, I looked him in the eyes. "I need to tell you something about me," I said. "I have not been honest with you."

The color drained from his face as he anticipated the worst. "I'm an addict," I confessed. You could cut the tension with a knife. His face was a mix of confusion, anger, and disgust. I had never felt so small and worthless as I did at that moment. There was no going back now; he knew the truth—I was damaged goods. I was no longer this perfect illusion he had built me up to be in his mind.

"What is it?" he asked. I looked down in shame and answered, "Heroin." The night was filled with crying and yelling and never-ending questions. The only thing he knew about heroin addiction was that it had killed some of his high school friends. Unbelievably, he decided he was going to stick with me through this. He was determined to fix me.

Unfortunately, he learned the hard way that you cannot fix an addict. Months passed in which he helped me try everything—methadone clinics, therapy, and programs. To no avail. I would try to quit only to immediately relapse. My emotions were all over the place. I would keep him up all hours of the night, acting erratically from either having too many drugs or not enough. I knew he was almost at his breaking point. I could see the progression of damage I had done on his mind and soul over the previous eight months. It was now or never. I had to get clean for him, and ultimately, for myself.

Detox and rehab were as bad as anyone would expect. My tolerance was incredible high because I had been using heroin and methadone at the same time. I was a very difficult and volatile patient. I would throw fits and cause scenes if I didn't get my way. I was running on no sleep and losing my mind. In rehab they had to sedate me because they were at their wits end, and so was I. It was a struggle for my life, filled with ups and downs, but I could finally see the light at the end of the tunnel. I was almost at my two-year sobriety mark. The amount of growth I had experienced in that time was incredible. My mind and body were, for once, at a stable and healthy place.

However, there was something nagging at my soul, an emptiness. I became very interested in learning new things about the world. I was searching to find out, "Who am I? What is the purpose of my life?" I consumed hours and hours watching YouTube videos on things ranging from politics to religion to conspiracy theories. I felt like everything I was seeing was pointing in one direction: to Jesus Christ. I started watching more Christian YouTubers. I researched the history of Christianity and looked at the evidence, and I also watched debates on religion.

At one point it was like God had flipped a light switch on, and I just knew without a shadow of a doubt that he was real. The whole world looked different. It was like I was seeing it for the first time. I felt an overwhelming sense of joy and comfort. I wanted to yell from the rooftops that I finally knew the truth.

I texted my mom that the Bible was real. I laughed to myself because I knew she probably thought I was going crazy saying something so out of my normal character. I had an unquenchable thirst for more information. I read for hours upon hours. Reading the Bible became a completely different experience. Things made sense this time.

After my initial period of joy, there was a time of grieving. I grieved over the sin I had committed. I was horrified at the realization that God had been there the whole time and saw and knew everything. I would sob and pray for hours, asking for his forgiveness. God then gave me peace that I was forgiven because of what Jesus had done for me on the cross. If God was able to forgive me, I had to forgive myself, too.

Ironically, as I grew healthier and stronger, things between Jason and me gradually grew worse. We were moving further away from each other to the point *where we no longer had anything in common and could not connect at all. He was drinking a lot and hiding a newfound drug habit of his own.*

The stress of the past few years had gotten to him, and I was afraid he was going to be lost forever. Adding to our rift was the fact that I had experienced being born again. My personality had completely changed, and my interests had done a 180. This just drove the wedge between us even further. I could feel the annoyance whenever he saw me reading my Bible. He constantly pointed out how I was different now, and he didn't like it. Things eventually came to a head, and we had a huge blowout.

It ended with him giving me an ultimatum: It was either him or God. I responded, "God will always come first." The next couple of weeks were excruciating, and I leaned heavily on God to get me through it. I was staying at my grandmother's house until I could figure out what was going to happen next with my relationship. I prayed that God would soften Jason's heart and redirect the destructive path he was on, but I had come to terms with the possibility that God wanted me to walk away for good. Jason's alcohol and drug use had started to spiral out of control, but over those few weeks, God had been working on him.

One morning I got a phone call from Jason. He sounded completely different. He had always been very prideful and never wanted to show weakness, but that morning he sounded absolutely broken. He asked if I would pray with him, which was shocking, coming from a self-proclaimed atheist. Where was his resentment toward my newfound faith?

Eventually, I felt it was right for me to go back home to him, but that meant new and strict boundaries starting with his drinking and drugs. He would have to prove to me that he was serious about getting clean. We had a bar hutch that was full of an assortment of alcohol. He suggested we get rid of every bottle, which is exactly what we did. The next day I removed every beer tumbler and booze bottle from the kitchen shelves and desk drawers; I even removed pictures from the wall that reminded either of us of our addiction. I confiscated all paraphernalia that felt wrong and brought them out to the curb on trash day.

I made it very clear that I was going to be following God and if that was something he could not handle, he needed to make his decision known. Thankfully, drug addiction wasn't the end of my story. I made it through to the other side to experience sobriety. My hope is that any knowledge I have obtained throughout my journey can be used to help someone else.

Hope is a wonderful thing. It fills all the nooks and crannies of a tattered and torn heart. Hope grows our hearts stronger. Light overcame the darkness in Victoria's life, and she stepped out of the life of addiction. Victoria didn't emerge *slowly* from drug addiction. The change in her was instantaneous and awe-inspiring. The light of freedom shone from her countenance as she proclaimed the Lord as her Savior. She is alive, vibrant, and changed. The resurrection power of Christ changed my sullen, angry, lifeless, resentful daughter back into the loving, sweet daughter we had missed so much! There are no words for the joy that filled our hearts.

Jason stood by Victoria. He provided stability and a safe place to continue her healing process. He proved himself to be steadfast and loyal, looking for the real Victoria emerging from the wreckage. Together they continued to grow and heal, building their individual lives and merging them together.

I rejoice with the promise of Hebrews 7:25 now fulfilled. Jesus interceded to the Father when I was in restless sleep, working, or just going about my day continuing to plead on Victoria's behalf. God spoke victory over Victoria's life and breathed new life into her heart. Victoria was able to break the cycle of drug addiction in her life. Her encounter with God was an internal tangible experience that created a dramatic change in her for all to see.

Joy returned to her features. Her thinking turned to be right-minded, and she developed an enormous thirst for the Word of God. God restored the love of reading to Victoria. This first love is the tool he is using to continuously fill her mind with life.

The beautiful letter from Victoria, which follows, shows that seeds of faith have grown roots and are blossoming in her heart. These seeds fell on good soil and are producing a fruitful crop. The words below are a treasure, which continue to live in my Bible today. My friend, I hope these words are an encouragement to you as well. As you read, envision this letter is for you, from your child. Despite what you see in seasons of struggle, your child loves you deeply.

Mom,

I know I'm not the most ideal child and that I make a lot of mistakes. But I want you to know that I am so grateful that no matter what you still love me unconditionally. You are the strongest person I know, and I hope and pray every day that I can be more like you. I don't know where I'd be if I didn't have you as a mother—if I didn't have your advice and support to lean on.

I'm sure sometimes you wonder why your children make such destructive choices. I think God gave us kids to you as our mom because he knew you would have the strength, patience, and love to save us and help us end up with good lives. I love you so much for never giving up on me. I know over the years it may have seemed like I didn't care because I pushed you away, but I want you to know that I never wanted to hurt you. I just couldn't bear the thought of disappointing you.

I love you very much, and I think you are an amazing woman and mother. I want nothing more than to make you proud.

Victoria

God promises the love of the Lord remains forever with those who fear him. His salvation extends to their children's children. Because I fear (reverence and honor) the Lord and have received salvation, I have the reassuring promise in Psalm 103:17 that my child's birthright is promised salvation. I can stand on God's promise. He is mighty to save.

Chapter 18

The Darkness Returns

Hope doesn't flee when the darkness starts to roll back in if it's a hope that's anchored in Christ. Darkness did start to roll back into Timmy's life. Why would anyone who has been set free choose to turn back into the pit of despair? I know that anyone who has lived through addiction with a family member asks that same question. Why would he turn back? The question haunted me. Timmy made the same wrong choices over and over again.

The answer can be found in the self-destructive cycle Timmy perpetuated. His skewed inner voice told him, "I'm no good, I'm a loser, I'm a failure." He listened to the lies and turned to find comfort and relief in the very place that compounded his problem. He turned to a fake savior. He turned back to the drugs.

One example of this cycle occurred when Timmy totaled my car during one of his alcoholic binges. This, in turn, increased his self-loathing. His response was to drown out the anger he felt toward himself with an increase in substance abuse. He continued to alienate himself instead of reaching out to people who could provide support, thereby increasing his loneliness. His stress level was palpable, increasing his anxiety. And the cycle continued.

One night, the Lord showed me a new vision of Timmy. The picture was as clear as if he were sitting in front of me; it tore my heart apart. This time, I saw Timmy kneeling, not in worship, but in dejection, with heavy weights upon him. These heavy weights were enormous, entangled chains holding him down. He could not rise up. The chains held him fast. His downcast face held an expression of despair. Waves of anguish seemed to roll off him. But then the image that I had seen in my first vision, which showed Timmy worshiping, slid in place next to this despairing image of him. The images appeared side by side.

Our days became even more painful as we watched Timmy decline again into the abyss. Sometimes, we're called to just breathe and put one foot in front of the other. We're always called to pray.

I believe the chains that held Timmy symbolized the many strongholds that kept him in bondage. His most damaging stronghold was his own feeling of shame. The truth in this paragraph from Christine Caine's book titled *Unashamed* resonates deep within my heart:

> *Shame loves silence. It grows in secret. The secrets we keep about our shame, or about the things that caused it, only intensify our shame. Keep shame a secret, and it festers. It thrives in the dark where our enemy lurks, wanting to keep us immobilized. We need to let God's light shine in those places.*[1]

Timothy struggled to believe God could break the chains that bound him. He believed Satan's lies over God's truth.

Chapter 19

The Unthinkable Happens

Solid advice pregnant women often hear is, "Sleep as much as you can now, because you're going to miss it." It's very true. Sleep is one of the first luxuries to disappear once you become a mom. It reappears just enough throughout the years of child-rearing to give you a taste of deep slumber, and then it vanishes into thin air again. In this season with Timmy, sleep was once again a valuable commodity in short supply for me. The apprehension that drove the hamster wheel called my brain would not turn off. I prayed, I pleaded, I fretted, and I prayed some more. Eventually, morning always came.

After weeks of being unable to shake the unease that we were living in, one night, I finally fell into a deep peaceful slumber. I didn't even remember lying down in bed the night before. All nightmare scenarios ceased. My mind stilled, and I slept for the entire night. This was an anomaly that had not happened in a very long time. Looking back, I realize that the Lord was giving me the gift of deep rest. He was preparing me for what was to come and giving me what I would need to face the morning. The third and final domino was about to fall.

Blow to the Soul

Abruptly at 5:30 a.m. a loud banging on the back door woke us up. Wayne and I both jumped up disoriented with our hearts racing. When Wayne looked out the window toward our driveway, he saw two police cruisers parked at the end. He turned to me and said, "This is it." People say time stands still when you're in a life-and-death situation. They're right. We knew what was coming. We stood frozen until the banging sounded again. The ruckus sent us flying down the stairs to the back door.

I felt like my brain split in two as Wayne opened the back door. One part of my brain thought, "H*ow can they possibly be police officers? They look like 12-year-old boys.*" Their nervousness was apparent as we stared at each other for a moment. My heart bled a little for the job they had been tasked with, while the other part of my brain just kept thinking, "N*o, no, no,*" which I muttered over and over as one officer spoke those fateful words: "We're sorry to inform you, but Timothy Peterson passed away last night."

No parent should ever have to hear those words spoken of their child. It's not natural for parents to bury their children. My already shattered heart found it was still possible to break further.

Sometime after around midnight, Timothy had driven to our old neighborhood. I wonder if he had gone to where he felt he was at home. Or was it just the convenience of finding his drug of choice easily? He pulled into the Price Chopper grocery store parking lot directly across from our former home on Cambridge Street and parked in the closest spot facing our old house.

He had taken his boots off and positioned the front seat of the van in a half reclining position and turned the radio on his favorite sports game. Then he shot up for the last time. Timothy overdosed. Was it intentional? Or could his body just not take any more abuse? Or had God said, *"Enough"*?

Philip Yancey, in his book *The Question That Never Goes Away—Why* says, "Grief is the place where love and pain converge."[2] In this family journey through addiction, I have been well acquainted with unconditional love, justified anger, heartbreaking sadness, bone-chilling fear, and debilitating anxiety. Now, I have met *grief.*

Standing in Hope

It's hard to explain what happened in my head that day. There was a lot of confusion. I didn't know what to do next. What do people do with an unexpected death? We had no experience with this type of tragedy. After our initial panic, we made difficult phone calls to Corey, Tanja, and Victoria. More calls to the many aunts and uncles. Family and friends jumped in to help with phone calls and Facebook posts. It didn't take long before everyone who ever met Timmy knew that he wasn't with us anymore.

I have no memory of what I might have said to anyone in the hours after answering that door. Over that first week of loss, I seesawed between craving solitude and needing family closeness. I craved solitude to bawl my eyes out and to yell at God, "Why? God, why!" I needed family to hug and talk through this incomprehensible happening. At the same time, I craved privacy to seek answers and peace for us all.

I think it's OK to be honest with God. After all, he sees what's in our hearts. There are no secrets between us and God. I believe he wants us to talk to him about everything. That includes our frustrations, anger, sadness, and confusion with unanswered prayers.

A calmness settled over my heart like none that I've experienced before. God's answer to me was peace. It sounds crazy. My heart was shredded, but I was at peace. I have learned that God is close when things are going well, and he is even closer when your life crumbles.

One of my favorite hymns growing up was *When We All Get to Heaven* written by Eliza Hewitt in 1898. The chorus says:

> *When we all get to heaven*
> *What a day of rejoicing that will be*
> *When we all see Jesus*
> *We'll sing and shout the victory*

The Bible clearly teaches that there is a heaven and there is a hell. The looming question in my mind and in the girls' minds was, "*God, is Timmy in heaven with you? Why didn't you save him?*" I didn't ask Him this question calmly and quietly. In one of those mornings of solitude, I had it out with God. I was loud. Tears streamed down my face. I was angry. I demanded assurance. I'm so grateful my heavenly Father wasn't offended when his daughter threw a tantrum. Instead he patiently loved me and waited. He waited for me to stop ranting and *listen*. My thoughts turned to my Bible.

Still with a rebellious attitude, I opened up my Bible. I rarely open up the Bible randomly, putting a finger on a verse and assuming that verse is what God is saying to me. God is not a genie in a bottle that we command at our whims. My preferred method of reading the Bible is with topic or plan in place. But this wasn't the time for a plan. That particular morning, I demanded he show me something, anything that would release the fear that was creeping around in my head.

I opened up to a spot where there was one of my many bookmarks, scoffing because I had landed on a pre-marked page. More tears fell when I noticed the bookmark was Timmy's first-grade picture from the First Assembly Christian Academy. When

I moved the bookmark to look at the page, I immediately noticed I had previously highlighted verses and through more tears, I read 2 Chronicles 33:12–13:

> *In his distress he sought the favor of the LORD his God and humbled himself greatly before the God of his ancestors. And when he prayed to him, the Lord was moved by his entreaty and listened to his plea; so he brought him back to Jerusalem and to his kingdom. Then Manasseh knew that the LORD is God.*

A persistent thought pressed into my mind after I read the scripture. *Read it again, and this time insert Timmy's name:*

> *In Timmy's distress he sought the favor of the Lord his God and humbled himself greatly before the God of his ancestors. And when Timmy prayed to him, the Lord was moved by his entreaty and listened to his plea; so he brought Timmy back to Jerusalem and to his kingdom. Then Timmy knew that the Lord is God.*

God spoke to me through his Holy Scripture. The peace that had started to slip a little began firming. Not wanting to misinterpret or misuse scripture, I dug a little deeper into what the Bible tells us about Manasseh. Manasseh was an evil king, but he eventually realized his sins and called out to God. God listened to his prayer and forgave him. God is a forgiving God. There is nothing we can do that is so horrible that it is beyond his forgiveness. If I could trust that God cared enough to seek out this evil king, then I could trust that he cared enough to seek out my son.

Chapter 20

Memorial Service

Pastor Brian Minnich began Timmy's memorial service with these words, "We are saved by grace through faith. It's a gift from God. Not based on any works. We're trusting that Timmy is now with his eternal Father. At eternal rest." Pastor Minnich went on to his opening prayer in which he thanked God for Timmy's confession of faith that Jesus is Lord.

During his memorial service, we played a transcript from a time when Timmy spoke at a Teen Challenge service at Valley Chapel in Uxbridge, Massachusetts.

Hi, my name's Tim Peterson,

I grew up at the end of Route 146 in Worcester. I grew up in the First Assembly of God Church in Worcester. I actually grew up going to Douglas Camp. I had a lot of family that grew up in this very church. My whole life I was in church. I was constantly fed the word from the Bible, but I never understood it. I never had a real relationship with Jesus.

I became attracted to drugs and alcohol. I felt uncomfortable with myself. I was insecure. I just never liked anything I did. And didn't get any joy in anything. I started getting high. In the beginning of my addiction, I got into a bad motorcycle accident. I was in a lot of pain almost every day. I used it as an excuse to just keep getting high and use more and more. It went on for a long time and, in the process, I hurt the ones I love the most, my family.

In January I got arrested. I made bail, but my parents didn't know what to do. They didn't want to bail me out because they felt I was safer in jail than out on the street. They thought I was going to die. They let me stay in there a little while to clear out my head and clear out my thinking. When they bailed me out I knew what I had to do.

I tried to go through teen challenge before, a few years ago. I was just doing it for all the wrong reasons. I wasn't trying to have a relationship with Jesus or anything. It's a hard program so I had ended up leaving early. I just couldn't do it on my own and that's what I was trying to do over and over again.

So, when I got out of jail I knew I had to go back there because the only joy I ever felt in my life was doing Jesus, you know. I went back in January, and I've been there for 6 months. I've never been happier in my life. I love it. It's a lot of work but it's the place where God wants me today. I ruined my relationship with my family, but restoration is happening. Every day it gets better. My family's here today.

The journey on the road of grieving is unlike any other. My brain functioned on autopilot after Timmy's memorial service. My emotions ran the gamut from bouts of tears to complete calmness. The outpouring of love and support from our close communities of church, family, friends and work were so very important to me.

I had not realized how much a sympathy card or note of encouragement could mean until then. I was amazed and humbled by the number of people who walked alongside us.

After one of my tear-filled mornings of lamenting Timmy's loss. God spoke to me. He simply said, "*I answered your prayer.*" This thought did not originate from my lamenting. I didn't see an answer to prayer. I only felt the gaping hole in my heart. I had prayed what seemed like a million prayers asking for healing, safety, and salvation for Timmy. "*Lord, which prayer did you answer?*" The persistent response repeated, "*I answered your prayer.*"

This was a sobering moment—it was a moment when I had a choice to make. Would I lean into Proverbs 3:5, which tells me that I could trust in the Lord and lean not on my own understanding? Or would I allow bitterness to grow in my heart?

I chose to leave Timmy in my heavenly Father's hands. I will not allow doubt or fear to creep in. I will not allow my vivid imagination to take hold and create horrible scenarios of suffering for Timmy. I will not dwell in self-recrimination. *I should have done more! We should have done more.* If I let all those thoughts live in my heart, then I am not leaving Timmy in my heavenly Father's hands, and then I have removed God from his sovereign throne.

I believe Timmy's chains are finally gone. He is set free. I believe he is now in heaven with both arms raised to his Lord. Tanja wrote a beautiful eulogy for her brother to bring some comfort to those who were suffering.

Tanja Speaks

My brother was a kind-hearted man who was fighting many battles throughout his life. Depression and anxiety are both powerful things that can take over your life in ways many people (even I) don't understand. Because of this battle, my brother turned to drugs and alcohol. It was his way of coping with the everyday struggle he was facing. He hated the drugs and fought day after day to get clean.

During this fight, a lot of you lost a great friend. Friendships were broken long before his life was lost. For that I am so very sorry. I find myself asking whether there was more I could have done to help him. So, I know that many of you are asking the same thing. Guilt is something that I am going to give to God. I'm going to trust in him to heal my heart and be with us during this time.

I believe that my brother is in heaven. I believe in a God of love and a God of forgiveness. I believe in a God who knows our innermost being and knows my brother's heart. This brings me peace during these dark days.

Chapter 21

The Aftershock

The months after our loss of Timothy are best described as the "twilight zone." Nothing felt normal. Our typical daily routine was disrupted, which in itself was a comfort. My thoughts and actions were unfocused. I walked in circles for days.

The most productive thing I accomplished in the two weeks after Timmy's death was to build a rock garden. It felt settling to work on the mundane task of carrying heavy rocks from behind our barn to the old patch of monster weeds. I found comfort in the simple task of planting baby plants among the rocks. Digging in the dirt and planting new birth proved to be therapeutic.

Wayne had always accepted every challenge and obstacle that came our way. But with the loss of Timmy, his world was turned upside down. Still he managed to do what he has done for over 40 years: He continued to walk forward in faith and provide for our family, friends, and customers. His rugged, scarred hands tell their own story—they speak of a man who has a deep conviction and commitment to carry on in the face of adversity.

Wayne and Corey, along with their crew, continued in steadfastness, doing what needed to be done. Timmy's floor jobs still needed to be completed, but without him, the process was much harder. At each job they faced painful reminders that Timmy was missing. Contractors and customers showed compassion and kindness in many ways. Upon one homeowner's request, Wayne inscribed Timmy's name as a memorial in the customer's partially completed subfloor. Without a doubt, Timmy left a gaping wound that will take many years to heal, and his acts of kindness and creativity are irreplaceable.

From behind our family's tears, a strength has emerged, and we are resolved that our steadfast faith will not be shaken. Although this terrible storm has rocked our world, we are determined to remain resilient.

Grief Support Group

A few months after we lost Timmy, a friend suffered the tragic loss of her son. Together, we joined a support group at a local church. If you are going through a difficult journey, I highly recommend that you don't go it alone. Walking through the weeks and months and even years after a loss can be overwhelming and possibly debilitating. There is so much to shoulder and learn on this journey.

In our support group, I began to understand the stages of grief. This caused me to relax into the journey. Instead of saying, "God why did this happen?" I was able to turn my thoughts to being intentional. What I was feeling was OK and even normal. There isn't a wrong or right way to grieve. Everyone's grief journey is different. However, the encouragement from others who were also suffering loss brought a form of peace. If they can move forward, then so can I. I couldn't allow myself to wallow in the pit of sadness and destructive thoughts.

Joining a support group gave me tools to pick up my heartstrings and rejoin my life. Supporting others who are living through loss helped me continue my own healing process. Galatians 6:2 tells us to carry each other's burdens and, by doing so, we fulfill the law of Christ. God our Father knows that we have need of each other.

Anger simmered underneath the grief. Anger was one of my first emotions to surface after the tears stopped. Through a Grief-Share group, I learned that, often, loved ones feel a sense of anger and betrayal at the deceased person. Yes, I can say with all honesty that I was angry at Timmy. I was angry with him for dying. I was angry that our whole family was hurting because of this tragedy. I was angry that despite everything we had done, he hadn't stayed clean. It was all his fault. We would never have the privilege of celebrating his wedding. I would never hold his beautiful children on my lap. His gentle smile would never grace my table again.

My anger was often aimed at myself or my husband. The "if only" thoughts can be hard to nix. Both of us felt a huge amount of guilt because of our perceived roles in Timmy's addiction and death. Talking about anger in the support group taught me that anger can be a major stumbling block. It festers and turns into unforgiveness, which in turn, leads to a bitter, hard heart. But if we turn toward forgiveness, we begin traveling on the path of healing. I needed to forgive Timmy.

God has never intended for his children to live under sharp wounds of anger and guilt. How simple it sounds on paper but in real life, forgiveness is hard and painful work. It's work that I had to do. It was my job to put effort into my own healing. An oft repeated saying in GriefShare was, "God doesn't move parked cars." I had to choose to forgive or not.

The Healing Power of Forgiveness

It can be hard to forgive a person when it's impossible to talk things through. I longed to have one more conversation, not confrontation, with Timmy. If only I could put my arms around him and tell him that I loved him one more time. Through tears, I forgave and also asked Timmy to forgive me. I'm going to believe that God sent those words to his ears.

One beautiful morning, as I drove to school, the Lord made me aware that I was still angry at Timmy even though I truly thought I had worked through this issue and put it to rest. As I drove, I recalled that the night before, a group member had asked for prayer. I perceived her dilemma to be of her own making. She was harboring some serious unforgiveness, and I could see that it was creating a stumbling block in her life. I started praying specifically that the Lord would show her that she needed to forgive her family member.

Then, clearly, the words came into my mind, *"And when are you going to forgive Timmy?"* It was one of those emotional ambushes that caused me to pull to the side of the road. God revealed to me the unforgiveness I still harbored in my own heart against Timmy. Colossians 3:13 teaches us to bear with each other and forgive one another. We need to forgive just as the Lord has forgiven us. Who am I to not forgive Timmy when the Lord our God has forgiven him? The action of forgiving set me free from a host of feelings God never intended for me to shoulder. Through the GriefShare sessions, I learned that "I can't change my circumstances, but I can be radically different within these circumstances."

I chose to start focusing on gratitude. Gratitude is a happy pill. I encourage you to try it. Start a gratitude list and see your mood start to lift upward. It's also contagious. The more grateful you become, the happier the people around you become. It's not possible to stay gloomy and downcast around people who are grateful. This is a terrific strategy for taking control of your emotions instead of letting your emotions control you.

Chapter 22

See the Works of His Hand – Victoria's Wedding Day

The arched iron gates lay open and inviting as we drove through to The Chanler at Cliff Walk in Newport, Rhode Island. Before us arose an elegant white mansion like the ones that live in a little girl's fairy-tale dreams. Inside this graceful mansion, a beautiful young woman was preparing for the long-awaited day when she would marry her Prince Charming. The day was the thirteenth of August. The year was 2020.

That was the wedding day of our youngest child, Victoria. A surreal feeling encompassed my heart as the business of preparations stole the afternoon. The two hairdressers performed amazing feats with our hair. Makeup was applied perfectly. And throughout the afternoon, little Liberty danced about the room in joyous glee, the excitement providing her music. The photographer flitted about, taking pictures of every precious detail.

My heart fluttered, and I blinked back tears as I watched Tanja and Victoria bend over their bouquets to fasten Timmy's picture to Victoria's bouquet. This same picture had been affixed to Tanja's bridal bouquet. Our hearts have been broken. We've lived through the indescribable pain of losing a son and a brother. We've also lived through the abundant joy of a daughter and sister being set free.

Through the breaking and in the mending, we have all grown stronger. This strength has not come from ourselves, but from trusting in the One who holds all our hearts. On that joyous day, we could show our love for each other and rejoice.

Even though rain continued throughout the day, pushing away plans for an outdoor garden wedding, peace flowed. Victoria walked in on her father's arm, and he escorted her to the grand fireplace where Jason waited. The little girl's dream of a wedding to her prince in a castle commenced. We know not what the future will bring, but we know our heavenly Father. In him we can trust and believe that he has plans to prosper us and not to harm us, plans to give us hope and a future. We know our heavenly Father.

Victoria Speaks

> It's funny that my siblings and I long to be in the country and escape from the city. Most kids who grow up in the country dream about one day moving to a big city. I guess, as the saying goes, the grass is always greener on the other side. To be honest, I don't really know what I want for the future; I'm OK with wherever Gods brings me. These last two years running a business with my husband, Jason, have taught me one thing: Together, as a team, there is nothing we cannot do.

Chapter 23

Reflections

The question of why all this happened has resurfaced many times while I have walked this journey. At first, it was an angry, tear-stained question. Over time, the word *why* has mellowed and taken on a different tone. Lately, it has become contemplative as I reflect on what I have learned as a parent that could help answer questions, such as these:

- What clues did we miss?
- What can I say to someone who is walking in my shoes?
- How can I help another mother or father down their broken road?

Gardening 101: Eradicate the Weeds

After we lost Timmy, I found solace in my gardens. Over the past three summers, we've been working to restore the pretty gardens that were hidden underneath years of neglect. In those gardens and popping up in a variety of places in the green grass, we've been fighting the invasion of a hostile weed. This is a weed that starts out as lovely green growth by sidling up beside plants, bushes, and trees. At first glance, it fills in bleak areas with beautiful greenery. But upon close inspection, the gardener finds it is an insidious destroyer. This weed winds its way around the plants, bushes, and trees overtaking them. It climbs and twirls until it stunts and chokes the defenseless plant. Eventually, the weed is victorious, and the plant withers.

When we dug out a large section of the garden, we learned that the weed's root system is an elaborate labyrinth that creeps underground for long distances undetected. The roots are strong and thick, holding on even when pulled with immense force. In order to win this battle, we will need to eradicate the weed's root system. But, just when I think I've got the upper hand, it rears its ugly head in another section of the yard. We must stay diligent and persistent in tending to the yard.

Similarly, the evil weed of self-hatred was a labyrinth of deceit that spun around Timmy's heart. It came in the form of condemnation. Its destructive root system was laid with negative words and thoughts, which he confessed daily against himself. This self-hatred hammered words of worthlessness into his mind daily. Words such as, *"I'm no good, I'm a failure, I'm stupid, I hate myself, I can't do anything right, I will never be worth anything, my life is hopeless."* Words of freedom and love were drowned out by Satan's lies. This negative self-talk turned into an intense self-hatred. In two powerful scriptures, we are told: *"For as he thinketh in his heart, so is he"* (Prov. 23:7 KJV) and *"The tongue has the power of life and death"* (Prov. 18:21).

When Timmy invited Christ into his life, his sentence of guilt was acquitted. He was deemed not guilty. However, he continued to allow the words of self-hatred to consume him. Timothy replaced truth with lies. His toolbelt was lacking the proper tools to combat those lies.

Lysa Terkeurst, the author of *It's Not Supposed to Be This Way* says: "To be able to run free, we must do three things:

- We are to throw off what hinders us.
- We are to stay free of the entanglements of sin.
- We are to persevere by keeping our eyes on Jesus, who is the author of our story of faith."[3]

Apply the Word of Truth

The word of truth gives us tools to fill our toolbelt to win battles. When we ask Christ into our lives, we are given a new identity, and we are transformed. A divine intervention takes hold of our hearts and minds; however, this is not a passive process. Romans chapter 8 tells us not to walk according to the flesh but by the Spirit.

We are called to take action, not to sit in the muck and mire we create in our lives. With Christ, we can pull out and eradicate the destructive weeds in our life. Our strongest tool is the Word. It will not be an easy battle, for we live in a fallen world. Ephesians 6:11 says that you can live victoriously if you *"put on the full armor of God, so that you can take your stand against the devil's schemes."* Again, I ask myself, *"If I could go back in time, what would I change?"* A very wise woman in my support group says: "Shh! Listen more and talk less." I would sit with Timmy and truly hear what's in his heart. My words would not condemn or criticize, but only encourage and empathize. It's hard to stop being the mom who's supposed to know what's right and wrong. It's hard to stop being the problem-solver and fixer in our children's lives.

As our situation grew worse, I found it difficult to speak out positive words because I was so focused on the issues at hand. But Timmy didn't need to hear what I thought was right and wrong in his life. He needed to hear, *"I love you"* and to know that he mattered. He was running on empty, and he wasn't recharging from a healthy source. When a person is sick, small doses of medicine over a long period of time is what's needed.

If you're in a similar situation as we were, I encourage you to put your own preconceived notions aside. Allow yourself to be open in dialogue and unafraid to change your own mind.

Dialogue provides an opportunity to replace those negative words with positive affirmations. Simply stating:

> "No, it's not true that you're worthless." "You are fearfully and wonderfully made." Claim it with me.

> "No, it's not true that you're a failure." "You can do all things through Christ who gives you strength." Claim it with me.

> No . . . that's not true! This is true . . . Now say it out loud.

This process sounds simple and easy; however, in reality it takes preparation and courage to enact. As the parent, we would need to be proactive in searching the Word for ammunition to fight those dreadful words that take hold and crush the spirit. We need to move forward with prayer asking the Holy Spirit to cause hearts and minds to receive the positive words. Changing a mindset, which has habitually spoken negative thoughts is a difficult task. But not an impossible one.

The Tools That Sustained Us

I ponder the questions, "*What can I say to someone walking in my shoes? What are the nuts and bolts that sustained me?*" Without hesitation, my answer is *prayerful worship*. Worship has been my cornerstone. Without fail, it has pulled me back from the brink of despair. Undoubtedly, it has sustained my mind and spirit. Absolutely, it has brought peace and joy into years that had no hope.

For me, worship is the process of seeking God and allowing his Spirit to grow me to be more like him. As with any process, it takes time. It requires intentional acts hour by hour, day by day, year by year. I've dug deep into my reservoir of perseverance. The tools I recommend in this process are:

- Reading God's Word as well as the works of inspirational authors
- Filling your mind with good thoughts
- Filling your ears with truth-filled music
- Staying in good fellowship
- Seeking joy ardently
- Wrapping it all in prayer

Reading God's Word

In the intentional act of worship, submerge yourself in God's Word. Make it the main course of your spiritual diet every week. When you hide his Word in your mind and heart, his Word will carry you when the storms blow in. The deeper you dig in your reading or listening, the stronger you will be in battle.

My favorite technique for Bible study at home has become studying a topic with a notable Bible teacher. This requires having a Bible you are willing to write in using highlighters, pencils, and pens, and it requires space. It also means a visit to the local Christian bookstore, which is one of my favorite pastimes. Prayerfully, search the aisles for a book that delves deep into the Word. The Holy Spirit will nudge you toward an author or topic. Often, I stay on one author or topic for an extended time. Your pastor can be a great resource for helping you make sound book choices.

Position yourself with both your Bible and the book you are studying next to each other. As you read the book, find the key related passages in your Bible. Study them further using the book's author as a springboard. Then, write notes in your Bible. I have found this partnering very effective in developing a deeper understanding of the Word and building reference sections in my Bible. This way I can retain the information I learn and refer back to it easily.

Instead of letting the books you are finished with sit on the shelf collecting dust, share them with friends and family. In my book circle the owner writes their name on the front page; then as we circulate the book, each person signs the book in turn. The book is always returned to the person whose name is at the top of the list. This is a wonderful way to build community.

> *Thy word is a lamp unto my feet, and a light unto my path.*
> —Ps. 119:105 KJV

Filling Your Mind with Good Thoughts

In my third-grade classroom, I begin the year with a social thinking activity using paper dolls. Students decorate their doll as themselves and then come to the circle. Next, I read a story in which the child is being picked on with horrible words spoken to and about her. As the child's self-esteem plummets, she grows to believe these terrible words about herself to be true. Each time something negative is said about the child in the story, the students wrinkle their doll.

Eventually, their doll is tattered, torn, and crinkled. Harmful words don't have to be spoken by others. We are often so destructive in our own thinking of ourselves that we do more damage than anyone else could. This object lesson gives a visual to each student, showing how negative words and thoughts do irreparable damage to their own heart and mind.

However, the object lesson isn't over. Next, the students take turns either apologizing or saying something positive to counter the negative words spoken to the girl in the story. Each time encouragement is spoken, the child attempts to smooth out their paper doll. The student learns that no matter how hard he or she tries to smooth out their doll, the damage they have done cannot be fully removed. There is always a consequence for our actions. We build a bulletin board with our paper dolls to remind us of this valuable lesson that our words and actions can build up or tear down.

> *Finally, brothers and sisters, whatever is true, whatever is noble, whatever is right, whatever is pure, whatever is lovely, whatever is admirable—if anything is excellent or praiseworthy—think about such things.*
>
> —Phil. 4:8

After we lost Timmy, I learned that feelings and thoughts have the ability to ambush me. These ambushes took the form of an overwhelming feeling of sadness or anger. They hit at the most inopportune times. They especially liked to jump in when I was in a low place in my day. An ambush has a debilitating effect. I've noticed self-destructive thoughts of self-condemnation or lack of self-worth come in the form of an ambush as well. They come when I make a mistake or just simply "blow it." They come with memories of regret. Once they come into my mind, they are difficult to remove.

The best tool I found for combatting ambushes was to literally speak out against them and proclaim that I am a daughter of the

King. I can replace my negative self-talk with God's thoughts about me. Christine Caine, the author of *Unashamed* says:

> *If there's one key to watching the walls in your life fall, to moving forward in freedom, to seeing the promises of God at work, then this is it: You must learn to believe the truth of God's Word over the facts of your circumstances. You have to look to God, not at everything around you. Only then can you see what's going on from his perspective. We have to see that wall torn down even before it is. We have to believe that God is faithful to do what he has promised (Hebrews 10:23).[4]*

Filling Your Ears with Truth-Filled Music

Sing those ambushes right out the door. Praise and worship music prove to be the tool of combat, which causes the enemy to run. An ambush cannot succeed when my hands are raised to the Lord:

> *Enter his gates with thanksgiving and his courts with praise.*
>
> —Ps. 100:4

Staying in Good Fellowship

We are not designed to live this life alone. God created us for relationships—with Him and with others. Even Jesus had his twelve disciples who were his intimate friends. Finding a support network will require some effort on your part.

As adults, it can be easy to have surface relationships through work and family. The close-knit friendships we developed through our childhood become distant and disconnected. Self-isolation is an enemy that creeps in when we live in a smaller and smaller circle of relationships. In self-isolation it is easy to allow negative self-talk and ambushes to mushroom. We all need those friends who are our confidants, who we can trust to always have our back. We all need prayer warriors in our lives who will weep with us in tragedies and rejoice with us in triumphs.

Meaningful relationships, unfortunately, do not just drop into our laps. When we're in dire straits and difficult situations, finding a support network that is the right fit will require work on your part. Be open to opportunities. Be ready to think outside your everyday box.

I was successful in finding my support network through the internet when I researched support groups in local churches. The group I found was just a few miles away from me, and I picked up the phone and connected. I also didn't go alone. A dear friend was walking through a similar heartache and together, we found understanding and companionship within this group. The people in the group understood our pain, and the facilitator skillfully taught and led, so that useless platitudes were not spoken. Instead we could relate to each other in compassionate discussion.

Don't sit alone in your heartache or disappointment. Turn and seek good counsel. Let the healing process begin. I am grateful I didn't shut down and shut everyone out.

Eventually, I knew I was ready to move on from this group. I felt God's call to open my own support group. A passion had developed in my heart to walk with other parents who are hurting. So many mothers and fathers bear the burden of guilt, shame, fear, and despair alone when their children turn to substance abuse. I turned to prayer.

After research, planning, and prayer, I used Victoria as a sounding board. I poured out my heart and shared ideas with her. I was taken off guard by her response. It more than surprised me; it thrilled me. She wanted to join me and co-facilitate the group. God had laid the same burden on her heart.

Within our church, we started a support group for hurting parents. Our season of healing continued as we planned and prayed about how to support other families. In the first year, we built beautiful, nurturing relationships with a small group of women. These mothers were walking through the fire of destructive patterns in their children's lives. In this intimate group we shared laughter and joy, found a safe place to let the tears fall, and prayed—always.

We are not meant to walk these paths alone. God calls us to use our gifts to help each other. Someone is waiting for the gift of support that you can supply. Find a network in which you can grow and help others to grow. During this pandemic season, in which I write, many activities have been canceled. Thankfully, our group grew. God turns all things for his good. He uses all avenues, even technology! My dear friend, continue to walk in faith and hope. With God all things are possible.

As iron sharpens iron, so one person sharpens another.
—Prov. 27:17

Seeking Joy Ardently

Happiness can last for a moment, a day, or even a season. The drawback to happiness is that it is dependent on our circumstances. So, if our circumstances are good, then we are happy. Throughout this journey, I had to change my focus from seeking happiness in my circumstances to seeking joy in all situations, including my trials. In my seeking, I asked the Holy Spirit to show me places where joy can be found. It's amazing! Joy can be found everywhere. You just have to look for it.

Creating "gratitude lists" is one tool in my toolbelt for seeking joy. Strangely enough, I utilize this tool a lot when I run. I love to run. I will never be the fastest, win medals, or be famous as a runner. But the longer distance I run, and the harder hills I climb, the longer my gratitude lists grow. Running is an activity where my mind is either held captive by my body, or it rises above the physical, and my mental strength takes over. The harder the run, the more detailed the things become on my list.

My list starts with the obvious, my family, and whittles down to the nitty gritty of each of their positive attributes. It progresses to things I see and why they are so wonderful. Once this attitude of gratitude has started, it's very hard to turn it off, which of course is a great thing. A gratitude list is an easy activity to do anywhere and in any situation. You don't have to become a runner!

What puts a fire into your belly? What is it that you just can't wait to do? What brings you joy? Too often I've put work, either career or housework, before things that brought me a more personal feeling of accomplishment. We all have a lot of responsibilities. Our days are filled with busyness. However, God has given each of us something special that can be an outlet in life's stressful times. Put aside time for that special activity that you're thinking about right now.

Our family has a passion for "forest bathing." We love to get out on a tall mountain or just in a network of trails to hike. Hiking can provide relief from weekly tensions and push away the pressures in our minds. When Elijah was six years old, Grandpa taught him his secret and ultimate relaxation position after logging many miles on the trails. It's aptly called, the "dead bug." Together, they find a smooth rock at the top of the mountain and lay on their backs. Next, they stick up both legs and arms. If possible, they lean their legs up against another higher rock so they're resting. Aah! It feels so good. The dead bug also has the positive side effect of producing smiles all around. I believe God wants us to have fun. After all, he is the creator of joy. What is it that brings you Joy?

This is the day that the LORD has made; let us rejoice and be glad in it.

—Ps. 118:24 ESV

Wrapping It All in Prayer

Most importantly, each day we are given is a special gift. Every sunrise, sunset, and all that lies in between is precious and to be treasured.

A gift given to someone you love is always wrapped with care and precision in the most appropriate paper for the occasion. The giver chooses paper carefully to match the gift recipient. We take care to create crisp folds, line up the paper, and tuck in corners. After the box is covered completely without gaping holes, it receives a final ribbon or bow and a thorough inspection. Will the recipient be excited and happy when they see this gift?

Typically, children's birthday wrapping paper is covered in superheroes. These superheroes exemplify powers of superhuman strength, regenerative powers that enable them to beat terrifying foes and live with a permanent safety barrier. These superpowers are versatile and can be used to free the hero from many tricky situations. Superheroes are often encased in invisible and impenetrable armor, which protects them as they go into inevitable battles. In these battles, they may be thrown through buildings and stomped on; in the end, they lay battle-weary and bruised. But they *always* get up. They rebound over and over again. Essentially, they are indestructible. They always, let me repeat that, they *always*, beat the bad guys! In the end, the superhero wins!

Prayer is your superpower that will give you superhuman strength. Prayer will regenerate your mind, soul, and body so that you will beat terrifying foes. Prayer is your permanent God-given safety barrier and your weapon to wield against the evil villain. Wrap every day from early morning through the night in prayer.

Pray without ceasing, bringing all things, no matter how small or big, before our heavenly Father. Take prayer into your battles and come out victorious.

Put on the full armor of God as instructed in Ephesians and you too will be indestructible. With Christ, you are a superhero:

> *Finally, be strong in the Lord and in his mighty power. Put on the full armor of God, so that you can take your stand against the devil's schemes For our struggle is not against flesh and blood, but against the rulers, against the authorities, against the powers of this dark world and against the spiritual forces of evil in the heavenly realms. Therefore put on the full armor of God, so that when the day of evil comes, you may be able to stand your ground, and after you have done everything, to stand. Stand firm then, with the belt of truth buckled around your waist, with the breastplate of righteousness in place, and with your feet fitted with the readiness that comes from the gospel of peace. In addition to all this, take up the shield of faith, with which you can extinguish all the flaming arrows of the evil one. Take the helmet of salvation and the sword of the Spirit, which is the word of God.*
>
> —Eph. 6:10–17

In those battles, follow the lead of Lori Wilkerson Stewart, the author of *Promises for Prodigals, One Hundred Biblical Promises to Declare Over Your Prodigal Guy*:

> *I did the only thing I could do—pray and stand on God's word. Scripture after scripture gave me hope. I underlined them, prayed them, and copied them*

into journals. The Word truly became my weapon, and I wielded my sword against the enemy with more expertise each day.[5]

I encourage you to find a prayer partner or group. In my connect group for hurting parents, we are sisters and brothers who will weep and grieve alongside each other. Because we share similar issues, we can understand and hold each other up in prayer. We can be honest with each other, providing a network of strength and support for one another. Together, we take opportunities to laugh as well as to talk and pray, seeking God's face for each other.

Grief can cause us to climb into ourselves. Helping others brings us back out again. Praying and studying God's Word together is a conduit for healing and comfort.

Look to the LORD and his strength; seek his face always.
—1 Chron. 16:11

Chapter 24

I Hear a Voice in My Heart

As I sit writing my thoughts, I've been watching my beautiful two-year-old granddaughter, Liberty Rose, from my window. She is the second apple of our eye. Wayne and I have the privilege to play with our precious grandchildren in our roles as Grammy and Grandpa.

Liberty is running with joyous abandon in the front yard with Corey and Kellie. Their beautiful daughter was born three months after Timmy passed away. James 1:17 tells us that, *"Every good and perfect gift is from above, coming down from the Father of the heavenly lights, who does not change like shifting shadows."* God knew that a sweet, loving little girl would help heal our family's hearts.

We can trust the timing of his gifts to be perfect. We can surely believe that he has a plan and is working all things together for our good. God has proven to me that he holds all our tomorrows in his hands.

Liberty giggles wildly as her father lifts her up twirling and swinging her around. She has total faith in her father. With complete confidence in the safety of his arms, she flies through the air. After the father-and-daughter romping ended, Corey walked away from her to sit on the porch. She immediately mimicked him, her adoring eyes on his every movement. When he rises to walk, she's on his heels dogging his every step. Her voice chanting, *"Da-Da."*

May we, as a family, learn to follow at the heels of our heavenly Father. May we turn our eyes on him only and trust him implicitly. With complete confidence may we know we are safe in his arms.

Emilia Grace, our third beautiful grandchild, joined our family April 6, 2021. She is a cuddler who loves a good snuggle. She is at the wonderful stage of baby discovery. Her smile breaks out like morning sunshine from ear to ear as she recognizes family. The simple things in life enthrall her such as toes and rolling over. We are truly blessed.

My friend, I've already introduced you to the first apple of our eye who joined our family on January 10, 2011. From our first moments together, Elijah stole our hearts. A delightful bond developed with Grandpa and Elijah as he crooned hymns to the fussy infant. Within seconds, Elijah would calm and fix his gaze on Grandpa's eyes. We fostered his love of music with Grammy's worship CDs at bedtime and any time we rode in a car together. The power of music continues to grow within Elijah. From the heart of my very precious grandson, I leave you with his first worship song:

I Heard a Voice in my Heart

I heard a voice in my heart
It was saying
as long as you believe me
You will have a forever lasting life.
Forever, forever, forever lasting life.

—Elijah Hodge, age 6

I hope the powerful message in Elijah's words brings you comfort and peace. We wait in anticipation and delight that many more songs will follow. This is my prayer for you:

Dear Friend,

My prayer is that you have met with Jesus while reading my story. My hope is to encourage you if your heart is aching. I pray you will take refuge in our heavenly Father. He will prove himself faithful in every situation you may be facing. When you're tempted to doubt him or distance yourself from him, I urge you instead to intentionally shift your thoughts toward him. Feed your faith daily with his Word. Apply that same Word over your family and in every situation that you face.

I pray you find safety, grace, and mercy as you open your heart. Do not allow fear or anger or any negative thought to take a foothold in your life. From the time you awake until the time you lay your head back on your pillow, trust that He is sufficient. The Lord will never fail you. Test him and see that he is good. You can find rest by placing your full confidence in the heavenly Father. "Look to the Lord and his strength; seek his face always" (Ps. 105:4).

Your sister in Christ,
Carol

Acknowledgments

I owe a debt of gratitude to my family: You have been my support system throughout this project. Thank you to my husband Wayne, and my children Corey, Tanja, and Victoria for your honesty and vulnerability in sharing your innermost thoughts. Listening to your memories has been precious and insightful. I am beyond blessed to call you my own. Thank you to my sister, Arja, who suffered through the first manuscripts, calmed my many doubts, and has been my sounding board. When my insecurities arose, my family continued to push me forward.

Thank you to the two wonderful, godly women who reentered my life to support this project. Nancy Robbie and Connie Goddard, you were an answer to my prayers. Your editing of my manuscript was an enormous boost that propelled this project forward. I will be forever grateful for the gift of your time and talent.

Thank you to Michelle Bates, author of *Beyond the Shallow— How Suffering Led Me to the Deep End of Grace,* for connecting me with the publishing company that finalized my project.

Appendix:
Questions for a Pastor

Dear Reader,

I first met Wayne and Carol, along with their two teenage sons and two younger daughters 23 years ago, when I became the youth pastor at their home church, First Assembly of God in Worcester, Massachusetts. I enjoyed their enthusiasm and sense of adventure, and I valued their commitment to church life.

Now I am the senior pastor of this same church, but with a new name, *Living Word Church*. My ministry for the past 28 years has involved serving on the mission field, on the college campus, and within the community and the church. My passion is for teaching, discipleship, and church-planting. My wife, Glorieann, and I have the honor of being parents of four children: two sons aged 19 and 20 and two daughters aged 13 and 14.

Carol asked me to write this appendix, "Questions for a Pastor," which contains common questions that arise in the process of parenting. As you read you will see responses that come from my heart as a parent, my experience as a pastor, and my knowledge as a Bible teacher. Far be it for me to simply share what I think—rather, I have done my best to break open God's Word, so that we can be healthier parents guided by grace and truth and filled with God's spirit and wisdom. I have reflected on many past conversations with Christian parents and the times I have led in prayer for wayward, hurting, and broken families. I have a heart to equip parents to stand in faith, practice their faith, and lead their sons and daughters toward lives of faith in Jesus Christ.

My thanks to Carol for being vulnerable with us, and my thanks to you for reading and reflecting on God's plan for parenting.

In faith, hope, and love,

Pastor Brian Minnich

Q1. What is the importance of home in our Christian faith?

Home is really important to our Christian faith. I'll start by saying, home is not the same as house. A *house* is a place, but a *home* is a people . . . people who give love, understanding, and acceptance. Home is where we belong!

A home doesn't have to be perfect to be a Christian home . . . in fact, perfection is impossible. Jesus was born into a home in which the circumstances of his birth were deemed by others as less than perfect. And later in life, we learn that Jesus's own brothers and sisters didn't really get the Messiah part of his life—at least not at first. But Mary and Joseph got it. And as parents, we can follow their example and try to understand our kids—their personalities, gifts, and callings.

Every Christian needs to know that faith practice in the home is the number one predictor of our faith being passed on to our kids. If our kids see us pray, hear us pray, listen to us sing to Jesus, and watch us serve others, they conclude that our faith is alive. Even better, when we take time to talk to our kids about faith and pray with them and bring them into our serving of others, they catch the faith!

As a pastor, I cannot stress this enough: Parents, please fill your home with love, understanding, acceptance, and prayer. Please practice your faith so your children can see it, hear it, and catch it. And if you have been failing or falling behind in any these areas, you are not alone. No home is perfect, but God is gracious. Ask for his forgiveness and help, and he will give it!

> *Lord, I want my home to be a place of honesty, a place of affection, a place where my kids feel safe to be themselves. Please help me love and listen and*

learn. Please forgive me for times when I took my kids to church on Sunday but neglected showing them my faith on Monday. Please help me make my home and my faith come together. Amen.

Q2. What is the role of influence and friends among our children?

There is no doubt that choosing good friends matters. First Corinthians 15:33 says, *"Do not be deceived: 'Bad company ruins good morals'"* (ESV).I have seen some really good teenagers choose good friends and come through their teenage years with flying colors. And sadly, I have seen some really good teenagers choose poor friends and fall into negative and destructive behaviors. So, what can parents do to help their children and teenagers choose their friends wisely?

I think early intervention is important. As a parent, sometimes we just know. We know the good from the bad, and we know the outcome before it comes about. So, I encourage parents to be hands-on, meaning once you know your kid is picking a good friend, encourage it! Find time to give them rides so they can hang out; meet the friend's parents and have plenty of conversations about how the friendship is going. Just as true, when we have concerns about the choice of a bad friend, step in! Let's warn our kids and work to limit the relationship or even close the relationship. Should we pray for our kids and their friend choices? Absolutely! The more we are engaged the better.

Lord, we love our children and grandchildren, and we want them to have positive friendships. Please give them discernment to choose wisely. Help them find friends who have Christian faith, similar morals, and self-respect. And Lord Jesus, please protect our kids from evil and give them friends who encourage what is good. Amen.

Q3. What is the role of freedom and control in our lives?

We serve an amazing God, one who makes us in his likeness and image. And because of that we are made with freedom of choice. I remember as a kid when my parents tried to make me eat sauerkraut, and I wasn't allowed to leave the table until I did. It turns out that I had a pretty strong will and would rather fall asleep at the table than eat the sauerkraut. As parents we may have found ourselves in similar situations, we want something for our children, but they do not want it for themselves.

Yes, as parents, our job is to set boundaries and teach our children right from wrong. But we cannot control our children, and we cannot keep them from exercising their own freedom of choice. Rather, we can influence them toward good choices. We can reward good choices, and discipline for negative choices. I choose the word *discipline* rather than *punish* because Jesus was punished for our sins and instructs parents to train and discipline their children, not to punish them.

Training a child or a teenager involves two very important things. First, we can set a good example for them to follow. The kids are watching and will learn a lot from our behavior, speech, and attitudes. Second, we can converse with our children. Personally, I think this is one of the keys to parenting. It involves asking questions of our children, listening to them, and then sharing our thoughts and views. Our children should have the freedom to safely speak to us, and as parents, we should have the patience and love to listen. For they too are made in God's image and likeness, and we all have a patient and loving God who listens to us.

Lord, thank you for making us in your image and likeness. Please make us more like you—more patient and kind and wiser. We recognize our freedom and our limitations in raising our children. Please give us the grace to train our children well by setting a good example and having open conversations with them, and please forgive us for the moments we have come up short. Pour your love into our hearts again. May we love our children the way you love us. Amen.

Q4. What is the role of scripture? How can we stand on God's promises?

HUGE! The role of scripture is huge. As parents we face decisions, pressures, and trials in raising our kids, so having direction and encouragement from God's Word is essential. I say essential, because we all have feelings, inclinations, and opinions that are subjective; but when we hear God's Word, we are hearing an objective view—the Truth.

For this reason, I read from scripture in nearly every meeting I lead because I don't have the answers, but God does. So, when I listen to a family and hear their needs, I prayerfully consider and ask God's Spirit for help in identifying a scripture that addresses their need. As a parent, you are the "pastor" for your family, so I encourage you to do the same. Identify the needs of your children, find a scripture that addresses the need, and then, stand on that scripture.

When I say, "stand" on the scripture, I mean several things. First, believe the scripture is true and speak it out loud. The more we hear it, the more we can understand it and believe it. Second, pray the scripture. It is a promise, a declaration, a commitment of God's truth, so pray and thank God for his promise. Third, as Deuteronomy 6:7–9 instructs, print scripture and post the scriptures around your house, your office, your computer, and your car—everywhere that catches your eye, so that you are reminded of what God says about your situation.

> *Lord, give us a passion for the Bible and build our faith as we hear your Word. We need your Word to speak to our situation so that we understand your promises and understand what is true. So, we pray, give us today our daily bread—we need the nourishment and counsel of your Word. Amen.*

Q5. How can unconditional love be stated and experienced in the home?

The unconditional love of God is what draws us to God. Romans 2:4 describes God's forbearing love in terms of a kindness, which ultimately leads us to repentance. We come to God in our weakness as sinners and find acceptance, but God's love is so powerful it not only accepts us as sinners, but it is powerful enough to transform us and not leave us in our sin. With God as our example, our first step as parents is to love our children while they are yet sinners. Unconditional love is just that: It is love given without conditions.

I encourage parents to express their love through lots of hugs and words of encouragement. Words have the power of life and death in them; they either build up or tear down. And when we choose to express words that bring life, we are literally shaping a positive self-image in our children, which they need to stand up to the negative speech all around them. As for hugs and physical touch, Jesus gives us a great example. He touched the children and blessed them! Positive words and healthy physical touch are essential for children to know and experience love.

I recognize that not all of us are comfortable with hugs and words of encouragement, but the reality is that our comfort needs to be submitted to the will of God. For God is love, and he commands us to love him and love our neighbors. Who is a closer neighbor than our own children?

> *Lord, we thank you for your love for us and for our family. Please give us courage and commitment to love our children the way you love us. Please shape our hearts to love with words and with physical touch. May our children find security in our love and may they find you, the eternal God, as the source of our love. Amen.*

Q6. What is going on inside us—the war within us?

There is a constant battle going on inside each born-again Christian. We have the natural urges of our first birth struggling against the spiritual urges of our second birth. All Christians face this struggle. No one is exempt. However, God knows this and is gracious to provide a way forward.

The struggle for the Christian looks something like this. When the scales of the struggle tip toward the Spirit, we rejoice and experience the fruit of the Spirit—love, joy, peace, patience, kindness, goodness, faithfulness, gentleness, and self-control. When the scales of the struggle tip toward our sinful nature, the Holy Spirit dwelling within us reminds, convicts, nudges, and draws us to repent, and we experience the fruit of repentance—confession, forgiveness, purification, wholeness, comfort, and reconciliation.

The bottom line is that being a Christian is about a relationship with Christ in which Jesus Christ has the final victory. The war is raging inside us now, but not forever. In the new creation, the new heavens and earth, the war between sin and spirit will cease, and the fruit of the Spirit will be limitless, and the victory of Christ will reign in us and over us. For now, let us acknowledge the battle within, be filled with his Spirit, and continue in God's grace. When we fall short, let us repent and turn again to our gracious God. We must not allow the battle within to sideline us from the battle around. As 2 Corinthians 12:9 states, his grace is sufficient, and his power is made perfect in our weakness.

> *Lord, there are moments in our lives when sin seems to reign in us. We need your grace. Please forgive us and draw us again to repentance, purify our hearts, and give us strength to fight this inner war. And Lord, strengthen us—we need endurance to continue this battle. And we pray for your victory now in our hearts, and we thank you for your eternal victory. Amen.*

As with all healing, emotional healing begins with an acknowledgement of our need. We need to be honest with ourselves and then express our emotional hurt to God. For if we hold onto our damaged emotions, there can be no healing—even worse, our wounded heart may grow, and the pain may increase. However, as we humble ourselves, pray, and share our hurts and desire for healing, we are essentially asking God to come in and be our healer. This is good and well within the power of God to do.

I think it is also healthy to share our hurt and pain with others whom we trust. For in so doing, we unburden ourselves and allow others the opportunity to be used by God to speak words of encouragement and healing to us. Not only does our wounded heart need healing, but often our emotional response to our wounds needs to be healed. By this I mean, our reaction to the pain inside us may be unhealthy and unholy. So, as we confess our emotional pain to God and to others we trust, we can also confess any sin that has arisen from the pain. Sometimes, we have become angry and bitter and unforgiving. Oh Lord, have mercy on us. Forgive us. Even help us forgive those who have caused the pain.

> *Jesus, thank you for being my healer. I am broken and in pain. My inner being needs your touch, your love, your wholeness. Relieve me of the anguish and revive me with your Spirit. Forgive me for holding onto the pain and for withholding forgiveness from others. I need you. Be my peace. Amen.*

Notes

1. Christine Caine, *Unashamed* (Grand Rapids, MI: Zondervan, 2016), 130.
2. Philip Yancey, *The Question That Never Goes Away—Why* (Grand Rapids, MI: Zondervan, 2013), 128.
3. Lysa Terkeurst, *It's Not Supposed to Be This Way* (Nashville, TN: Nelson Books, 2018), 131.
4. Caine, 156–157.
5. Lori Wilkerson Steward, *Promises for Prodigals, One Hundred Biblical Promises to Declare Over Your Prodigal Guy* (self-pub., 2018), 6.

CPSIA information can be obtained
at www.ICGtesting.com
Printed in the USA
BVHW090848040522
635996BV00045B/4277